AF531759

CULTIVATION TECHNOLOGY OF HOUSE PLANTS

By

Dr. Shubhrata R. Mishra

Deptt. of Botany
Vikram University
Ujjain (M.P.)
(India)

DISCOVERY PUBLISHING HOUSE PVT. LTD.
NEW DELHI-110 002

Published by:

Tilak Wasan

DISCOVERY PUBLISHING HOUSE PVT. LTD.

4383/4B, Ansari Road, Darya Ganj
New Delhi-110 002 (India)
Phone : +91-11-23279245, 43596064-65
Fax : +91-11-23253475
E-mail : parul.wasan@gmail.com
discoverypublishinghouse@gmail.com
web : www.discoverypublishinggroup.com

First Edition: **2014**

ISBN: 978-93-5056-410-3

Cultivation Technology of House Plants

Printed at:
Dynamic Printers
Delhi

Preface

Most house plants are hybrids of plant species that grow wild, somewhere in the world. A good rule of thumb for keeping your house plants healthy is to try to match the same environment from which they originated. You may not be able to match every criterion for your house plant, but every small step you take to ensure the plants comfort will be a giant step towards keeping them healthy.

Most house plants should be thoroughly soaked as soon as the soil dries during periods of active growth. Some plants, however, must never be allowed to dry out completely. There are no hard and fast rules to watering, because every situation is different, due to temperature variations, humidity and soil types etc. It is better to keep an indoor plant on a slightly dry side than over watered. More house plants die from over watering than any other cause! Never allow your house plant to stand in a saucer of water for more than an hour or two!

City water is treated with chemicals for your safety, however most house plants don't like chlorine or fluoride, so it's a very good idea to allow the water to sit in an open container for at least 24 hours prior to using it for watering. This is enough time for the chemicals to dissipate and evaporate from the water and bring the water up to room temperature.

Plants requiring medium light conditions (that will grow and bloom under a Gro-Lux light) include Achimines, Abutilon, fibrous Begonias, Cyclamen, Episcia, Impatiens, Primrose, and Sinningia and Hypoestes. Pretty much all green foliage plants, like Asparagus Ferns, will grow under a combination of cool and warm white household fluorescent lights.

Plants that require high, intense light (they need wide-spectrum growing lights if you do not have a very well-lit place for them) include Cacti and other succulents like the Sempervivums, Calceolaria, Calla, Senecio, Fuchsia, Geranium, Kalanchoe, Lantana, Linaria, Nemesia, Orchids, Passiflora, Schizanthus, and Streptocarpus.

If the leaves turn downward or look sunburned, they are getting too much light, and the light needs to be raised or the plant needs to be moved farther away from the light. If the plants stretch upward and do not flower as they should, this is an indication that they need more light.

—Author

Contents

1

Introduction

Essentially, growing indoor house plants requires much the same pot, soil, and planting preparation that a pot plant grown outdoors does. There are differences, however, so I'll list the basic requirements, even though they are similar to those for outdoor container plantings.

Use the Right Size Container!

Indoor plants do not need as big a pot as outdoor-grown plants, because they tend to grow much more slowly. You still, however, need a pot at lest twice the size of the root ball of your transplant, and if the plant is very immature, allow 4 to 6 times the size of the root ball. Of course, this does not apply to those plants that like to be pot bound in order to bloom – Amaryllis, Clivia, Orchids and Rex begonias are examples of plants that won't bloom or do well unless pot bound.

A Good Watering System

Bottom watering is generally best for pot plants, discouraging disease, and keeping the potting mix evenly moist. A self-watering pot with a water reservoir in the bottom works well, and, indeed, is the best way to grow African Violets, which don't like to be handled or splashed. A saucer under your pot also works well for bottom watering, for you simply pour water into the saucer and let capillary action pull the water up into the pot through drainage holes. You can optimize bottom watering by placing a wick of felt or water-conducting cord in the bottom of your pot when planting, and letting the end extend down into the saucer to help move water up into the potting mix. If you water from overhead, a watering pot with a long, small spout is good for controlling where the water goes, and keeping it off the leaves of your plant. Another way to provide bottom water and also humidity is to select a metal tray (copper is pretty and will not rust), fill the bottom with a layer decorative pebbles and place your pot or pots on top of the pebbles. Fill the tray with water to the bottom of the pots. This will not only water your pots, but also provide evaporation to humidify the air around your plants.

Good Drainage

This is the other part of proper watering. Yes, a container can have too much water! There are probably more plants killed with over watering than from any other cause. A few plants (Juncus, some of the carnivorous plants, anything that likes boggy conditions) do like to have a little standing water at their roots, though most plants' roots rot in such situations. Other plants like to be extremely dry and pot bound, such as Orchids and Clivia. For most plants, however, the ideal is an evenly moist, but well-drained soil! Evenly moist generally means that you water when the top inch of the medium is dry to the touch. If a plant likes to be dry between waterings, let almost the entire pot dry out before watering, though you should never let it go bone dry.

Humidity

Most plants like humidity between 30 per cent to 50 per cent. The watering system of pebbles in a tray filled with water helps provide good humidity. You can also have a humidifier in the room with your pot plants, and if you place your plants in a group (but not touching), this will also help keep humidity up in their vicinity.

Good Air Circulation

Do not crowd your house plants close together, but leave a little space between them. They need plenty of gentle air circulation to lessen the chance of disease and to help them get plenty of carbon dioxide, which they need for photosynthesis. Be sure the air movement is gentle; a cold draft can stress your plants and cause them to lose leaves. Be careful of opening a window near your house plants in the cold of winter, and also of placing them in the direct line of air from your air conditioner in summer. A humidifier will also generate some air circulation, while providing moisture that house plants need.

Plenty of Nutrients

The plant has no means of getting nutrients except from the growing medium in its pot, so you will have to feed your indoor plants with plant food. As long as the plant is blooming or in active growth, you can feed once a month with full-strength fertilizer (carefully follow the label on whatever fertilizer you choose). However, you will have more even results if you feed every two weeks with a ½ strength solution, or every week with a ¼ strength solution. Most fertilizers have salts, and if you see a whitish buildup on the rim of the pot or on top of the potting mix, you should flush the soil out with water for at least half an hour, or better, yet, discard the soil in the pot and start over. Of course, you can avoid this concern by using a natural plant food like Algoflash for Houseplants, which has a 100 per cent natually occurring mineral base.

Some plants bloom best if somewhat starved for nutrients, and if given great growing conditions will produce lots of foliage, but not many flowers.

Preparing Your Container

Choose a container with a drainage hole in the bottom, or a self-watering container, which will have the drainage hole(s) incorporated in the inner pot. You may want to line the bottom of the pot with irregularly shaped stones to further promote good drainage (though this should not be done with a self-watering container!). Be sure the drainage holes are not obstructed. You might have to check them periodically to be sure they are not blocked. If you use a decorative pot with no drainage holes, use it only as a cache-pot and place your plant, pot and all, into it (this is called double potting). Be sure to drain any excess water from the outside pot after watering, unless you are growing a bog-loving plant, such as Juncus, that loves to sit in an inch or so of water.

Use a soilless medium like park's container potting mix, which will provide your plants the proper drainage and tilth. Mix timed-release fertilizer into the potting mix according to the instructions on the fertilizer container.

Place the potting mix in a plastic tub or bucket and slowly add water while gently mixing, until the growing mix is moist but not damp. Add the moistened mix to the container until it is ¾ full. Remove the plants from their pots or communal tray (break up the sides of the root balls with your thumbs if they are pot-bound) and set the plants in the mix. Then add more potting mix until it is within 1 to 2 inches of the brim and tamp it down lightly. If the plants are small relative to the new container size, plant them at the same level that they were in their pot, so the top of the soil in their original pot is at the same level as the soil in the container.

Water Thoroughly

Provide Enough Light Plants use blue to violet light to produce foliage and regulate respiration, and orange and red light for growth, maturity and flowering. You can use fluorescent household cool white light (strong in blue and green) combined with household fluorescent warm white light (strong in red and orange) for plants with low to medium light requirements. If you need high intensity growing lights for plants that need a lot of light, there are a number of plant lights on the market that come close to providing the full spectrum normally provided by the sun, containing the correct amount of blue, red and far red for plant life. Some plants, like Clivia, do perfectly well in low light conditions. Others need plenty of light to perform well. Particularly in winter, if you have limited light or small windowsills, you should consider supplementing your natural light with growing lights if you want your indoor plants to look their best. A fluorescent light garden can be placed pretty much anywhere, since you don't have to rely on natural light from a window. Under a shelf, on a bookcase, on a kitchen counter or on a table in your den or bedroom can all become a mini-garden in your house.Plants to grow in low or indirect light include Clivia, the Rex Begonias, African Violets, and Philodendrons. They will all tolerate fairly low or indirect lighting conditions, though they will perhaps be more full and robust with more intense light.

Plants requiring medium light conditions (that will grow and bloom under a Gro-Lux light) include Achimines, Abutilon, fibrous Begonias, Cyclamen, Episcia, Impatiens, Primrose, and Sinningia and Hypoestes. Pretty much all green foliage plants, like Asparagus Ferns, will grow under a combination of cool and warm white household fluorescent lights.

Plants that require high, intense light (they need wide-spectrum growing lights if you do not have a very well-lit place for them) include Cacti and other succulents like the Sempervivums, Calceolaria, Calla, Senecio, Fuchsia, Geranium, Kalanchoe, Lantana, Linaria, Nemesia, Orchids, Passiflora, Schizanthus, and Streptocarpus.

If the leaves turn downward or look sunburned, they are getting too much light, and the light needs to be raised or the plant needs to be moved farther away from the light. If the plants stretch upward and do not flower as they should, this is an indication that they need more light.

One final word about growing under lights concerns the length of time the lights should burn each day. An automatic timer is very helpful in providing the consistent lighting conditions the plants need to flourish. As in nature, different plants require different amounts of light. Following are some general guidelines:

- Seed flats of annuals, vegetables, herbs and perennials can be lighted for 12 up to 24 hours a day until germination occurs, after which the light should be 12 to 14 hours a day.
- Most house plants like 14 to 16 hours of light a day when flowering.
- Foliage plants do well under 12 to 14 hours of light a day.

Some plants are affected by photoperiodism. This means they will bloom only when their requirements of darkness are met. Plants that like short nights (this means they get 14 to 18 hours of light a day), include tuberous Begonias and some annuals. Plants that like long nights (they need only 10 hours of light per day to flower) are much more numerous. Some of the long-night plants are: Cineraria, Leucanthemum (Chrysanthemum), Cyclamen, Kalanchoe and Gardenias.

Most house plants are hybrids of plant species that grow wild, somewhere in the world. A good rule of thumb for keeping your house plants healthy is to try to match the same environment from which they originated. You may not be able to match every criterion for your house plant, but every small step you take to ensure the plants comfort will be a giant step towards keeping them healthy.

The most important elements needed for indoor plant health are water, light and fresh air. Most plants have dormant and active cycles, and their watering and fertilizing requirements will differ greatly from season to season.A little research should be done for each of your House Plants to understand their individual needs.

Watering your House Plants

Most house plants should be thoroughly soaked as soon as the soil dries during periods of active growth. Some plants, however, must never be allowed to dry out completely. There are no hard and fast rules to watering, because every situation is different, due to temperature variations, humidity and soil types etc. It is better to keep an indoor plant on a slightly dry side than over watered. More house plants die from over watering than any other cause! Never allow your house plant to stand in a saucer of water for more than an hour or two.

City water is treated with chemicals for your safety, however most House Plants don't like chlorine or fluoride, so it's a very good idea to allow the water to sit in an open container for at least 24 hours prior to using it for watering.

Lighting Requirements for Your House Plants

The amount and the intensity of the light that the plant receives dictates much of a plant's life cycle.

Even though a plant species that may have originated in a jungle where it thrives in the shade of trees, appears to be getting plenty of light, the intensity of the light indoors may be much lower than what the plant actually needs. Insufficient light usually manifests itself with paler foliage, lanky growth, and general lack of luster. When this happens you must do whatever you can to increase the light intensity for that plant.

This can usually be rectified by moving the plant closer to the window, or moving it to another room with different light exposure. When you change the light drastically for a house plant, do it gradually to accustom them to the brighter light. Plants will sunburn if they are put into too bright of a light after their skins have become tender from lack of light.

Plants should never be placed between a curtain and the window if the nights are cold, even if they are sun lovers. It is better to have a sheer curtain that will admit the light, and have the plant in the heated area.

Growing House Plants under Artificial Grow Lights

It isn't necessary for your plant to even know that it is winter. You can dictate many of your plants functions by giving them supplemental, artificial light. There are 'grow lights' on the market today that successfully imitate the same light spectrum of natural sun.

These flourescent lights aren't perfect, and if they are the sole source of lighting, it will be necessary to have them on for 12-16 hours each day. It is a good idea to have them set on a timer so that the light hours are regular. If your intent is just to fool your plant into thinking that it is a certain season for blooming or whatever reason, you can set the timer to come on as the light begins to fade, and make your house plants day as long as you'd like.

Many flowering and foliage plants actually grow and look better indoors when grown under artificial lights. Keep in mind that plants like to rest now and then too, so if you are using growing lights, cut back the hours now and then and let your plants have a temporary period of dormancy.

Periodic Dormancy Needs of House Plants

Plants sense the natural shortening of daylight hours and may go dormant as they would in their natural habitat. This is usually a time when the amount of watering is decreased. On the other hand, many plants actively begin to grow or bloom, so they must have more water, and be fed. While plants are dormant they should only receive a minimum amount of water each time and only then if the soil becomes dry to the touch an inch below the surface.

Temperature, Humidity and Fresh Air Requirements for House Plants

Proper lighting and watering are, by far, the most important criteria for the health of your house plants, but temperatures and humidity will drastically affect your plants health as well. House plants, even though they may be of a tropical nature would rather sacrifice a few degrees of temperature in the home than the moisture in the air which they need to survive. Even though your plant may *prefer* a warmer situation, it sometimes comes down to accepting the lesser of two evils; *cool temps or lack of humidity*.Heated rooms, by nature tend to be dry rooms, especially if they are heated with forced air, or fire.Even rooms that have steam or hot water radiant heat will be somewhat dryer.If you want your plants to succeed, keep your temperatures as low as possible, while still remaining comfortable for yourself, but never below 50°. Generally, tropical plants enjoy a relative humidity of 50-70 per cent and warm emperatures. Unfortunately, when temperatures in the home rise above 67° F, the humidity drops drastically, so it may be necessary to sacrifice a few degrees of warmth in lieu of an increase in the humidity. Provide additional humidity by setting the plants on shallow trays filled with moistenedpebbles, a humidifier or aquarium, especially during the winter months. Frequent misting will help considerably.

Keep in mind that because glass is a poor insulator, the temperature near windows will be considerably colder. At night, be sure to close the drapes or move the plant to a warmer part of the room.

If you're trying to grow houseplants indoors, you'll find that some rooms of your house are low in natural light. Sunlight is the perfect balance of wavelengths necessary for plant growth and blooming, but you can also use artificial light to help your plants along. In fact, low-light foliage plants (such as pothos and peace lily) can grow quite nicely in windowless offices with enough artificial light.

In order to grow, plants need:

- Blue wavelength light for foliage growth.
- Red wavelength light for flowering and fruiting.
- Plants have little use for green wavelengths and reflect them back, which is why leaves appear green.

Types of Artificial Lights

For serious indoor growing and starting plants from seeds, you'll need hanging tube fixtures placed right over your plants. You can buy special grow light kits that include fixtures and reflectors, but for regular houseplants you can really use any lamp or light fixture as long as you choose the bulbs carefully and place the lamps where your plants can benefit most.

Artificial Lighting

- **Fluorescent lights** are by far the most economical and easy choice for houseplants. They come in tubes or compact bulbs (CFL) that screw into regular lamp sockets, and they're cool enough to put close to plant foliage. Generic fluorescent tubes and bulbs are higher in blue wavelengths, so look for "full-spectrum" or include a mix of "cool" and "warm" bulbs. When in doubt, buy "cool white" products, since white light contains the full spectrum of wavelengths. For maximum effect, position fluorescents about a foot away from plant foliage.
- **Incandescent lights** give off a lot of heat and should be placed farther away from plant foliage. Incandescent bulbs give off more red wavelengths, so they can be used to supplement fluorescent light and balance out the spectrum, especially if you're trying to encourage plants to bloom. If you want to mix the two, try using a ratio of about one-third incandescent and two-thirds fluorescent by wattage.
- **LED lights** are also a low heat, energy-efficient artificial light source. Because LED technology is so customizable, every bulb is different, so make sure your bulbs produce the blues and reds necessary for plants. Horticultural LED grow-lights produce only the wavelengths most utilized by plants, so you may want to look for these bulbs rather than buying ones for general use.
- **Halogen lights** can also provide full-spectrum light, but like incandescents they put off a lot of heat and are less energy-efficient than fluorescents.
- **Horticultural grow lights** are generally packaged in tubes for fluorescent fixtures. They contain the full spectrum of wavelengths needed for blooming plants such as African violets. Some gardeners find them useful when starting seeds or propagating hybrids, but others find that simple full-spectrum fluorescents work just as well.

Easy plant lighting for room with low natural light:

- Find a standing lamp with three bulbs, ideally one with moveable or gooseneck fixtures.
- Use one incandescent bulb and two compact fluorescent bulbs of the highest wattage you can, within the safe wattage rating for the fixture.
- Aim the lights toward your plant table. If each fixture is separately movable, then put the fluorescent bulbs closer than the incandescent, to avoid heat damage.
- Place a mirror or other reflective surface underneath your plants, to reflect light back up onto the foliage.
- Attach a timer set to 16 hours per day.

2

Aluminum Plant

Botanical Name: *Pilea cadierei*

Showy, silver-splashed leaves make Aluminum Plant a stunning and popular house plant. It's easy to grow, too, as long as you can meet its need for humidity.

Pilea cadierei is a fast-growing perennial plant. It spreads rapidly in its tropical native habitat, where it grows as a groundcover. Tiny, light-coloured flowers sometimes appear in summer. Don't be afraid to pinch them off. They're insignificant compared to the foliage.

Its ovate green leaves are about 3 in (8 cm) long. Silvery streaks mark each leaf, adding a dramatic metallic design to its quilted texture. These unusual patterns give this plant another common name, watermelon plant.

Pinch off growing tips to keep the plant from getting leggy. Pinch the fleshy stems early and often to encourage them to branch out and to stay compact. Don't toss out those cuttings, either. They'll root easily.

Aluminum plant prefers humidity to wet soil. In fact, it won't tolerate soggy soil which causes root rot. Aim to keep the soil lightly moist during the growing season.

Older stems will drop its lower leaves. This is normal. Cut back older stems in spring when they become leggy. If your plant drops quite a few leaves, it's likely caused by overwatering. Move the plant to a warmer spot and stop watering until the soil dries out a bit. If you believe you've hopelessly overwatered, repot at once in fresh soil.

- **Repot in spring** when it outgrows its pot. Use a pot with a hole to provide good drainage.

Plant Care Tips

- **Origin:** Vietnam
- **Height:** Up to 12 in (30 cm)
- **Light:** Bright light. The foliage will lose its variegation if the light level is too low. It's a good idea to place it in bright, filtered sunlight year-round.
- **Water:** Keep soil lightly moist spring through fall, slightly drier in winter.
- **Humidity:** Moderate to high humidity. To raise humidity, place the plant on a tray of wet pebbles. This plant also loves to be misted with room-temperature water. It makes an ideal terrarium plant.
- **Temperature:** Average room temperatures 60-75°F/ 16-24°C.
- **Soil:** Any good potting mix.
- **Fertilizer:** Feed every 2 weeks in spring and summer with a balanced liquid fertilizer diluted by half.
- **Propagation:** Take 3 in (7.5 cm) stem tip cuttings in spring or summer. Cut the stem just below a *node* — the place where a leaf is attached. Place the cut end in moist potting mix and cover the plant with a plastic bag to retain humidity. Cuttings root easily in a month.

3

Arrowhead Plant

Botanical Name: ***Syngonium podophyllum***

Arrowhead Plant is a member of the Araceae family — along with the philodendron — and is just as easy to care for. Give it bright light and lightly moist soil, and you'll find that it's otherwise low-maintenance.

Commercial growers have made big improvements to this beautiful foliage plant in recent years, giving it a better resistance to disease. And that's not all. Today's plants offer more leaf colours with heavy variegation and a compact growth habit, adding to its appeal.

As a young plant, its leaves start out heart-shaped, then gradually become arrowhead shaped as it matures. Its dark-green leaves have silvery white or cream variegation, making this a decorative and popular house plant.

Display arrowhead plant alongside a group of other foliage plants or add it to a dish garden. Small plants mix well with compact dieffenbachias and heartleaf philodendrons because they require similar care.

Young plants form clusters of upright stems, with climbing stems developing later. Use a moss stick to support older stems, giving aerial roots something to hold onto.

- **Pruning tip:** To keep arrowhead plant bushy and full, prune out the older, climbing stems as they grow. Cut them back in early summer and you can propagate the stem tip cuttings.
- **Dropped or shriveled leaves?** Arrowheads are always growing new leaves, but may drop them if the plant gets too dry. Cut off dry, shriveled leaves and aim to keep the potting mix lightly moist at all times.
- **Repot in spring** every couple years, or when the plant becomes root-bound.

A Note of Caution

The sap in this plant contains calcium oxalate crystals and is toxic to pets and people and can cause skin irritation. Researcher recommends wearing gloves when handling this plant or washing hands thoroughly afterward.

Plant Care Tips

- **Origin:** South America
- **Height:** Newer compact varieties grow to 2 ft (60 cm), some varieties climb to 4 ft (1.2 m) or more.
- **Light:** Bright light, but no direct sun. Can tolerate low light, but the leaves may lose their variegation. Turn pot regularly for even growth.
- **Water:** Keep the potting mix moist in summer, allowing the surface to dry out before watering again. Water less often in winter, letting the top half of the potting mix dry out.
- **Humidity:** Average room humidity.
- **Temperature:** Normal room temperatures. 60-75°F, 16-24°C
- **Soil:** Any good potting mix. Use a container with good drainage.
- **Fertilizer:** Feed every 2 weeks from spring through fall with a balanced house plant fertilizer diluted to half the normal strength. In winter, feed monthly.

- **Propagation:** Take 3-4 in (7.5-10 cm) stem tip cuttings early in summer. For best results, dip the cut end in rooting hormone powder then stand the cutting in a pot of perlite or a half-half mix of vermiculite and peat moss. Keep the cuttings out of sunlight and maintain the humidity around them by covering the pot with a plastic bag. Cuttings should root in about a month.

4

Asparagus Fern

Botanical Name: *Asparagus densiflorus* 'Sprengeri'

Asparagus Fern is not a true fern, but a member of the lily family (Liliaceae).

Long, arching stems densely covered with short, needle-like leaflets give this plant a delicate appearance. It has a cascading habit that makes it ideal for a hanging basket.

Mature plants will bloom in summer with small, white-to-pale pink flowers, sometimes followed by clusters of green berries that turn red in the winter. These berries are poisonous if eaten.

Florists love the feathery, emerald-green foliage in bouquets. It's also a popular outdoor container plant in temperate climates. If planted in the ground, asparagus ferns are invasive. In their native habitat, these vigorous plants will spread across — and scramble up — other plants.

- **Prune it back:** Trim off old stems in the spring to make room for new growth and to keep the plant looking neat.
- **Repot in spring:** Move to a pot only 1 size larger. Allow 1-2 in (2.5-5 cm) from the surface of the potting mix to the rim of the pot. The fleshy, tuberous roots sometimes force the potting mix up as they grow.

- **Leaf drop** is usually a symptom of too much sunlight—or, more likely—dry soil. Keep your asparagus fern where it'll get filtered light. Water regularly, but take care not to overwater. The plant's thick, tuberous roots store water and soggy soil can cause root rot.

Plant Care Tips

- **Origin:** South Africa
- **Height:** Trailing stems up to 3 ft (90 cm) long
- **Light:** Bright light.
- **Water:** Water thoroughly, allowing soil to dry out a little between waterings. Water sparingly in winter, but do not allow soil to dry out completely.
- **Humidity:** Prefers moist air. Set pot on a tray of wet pebbles and mist leaves daily with room- temperature water.
- **Temperature:** Average room temperatures 60-75°F/ 16-24°C.
- **Soil:** Peat moss based potting mix.
- **Fertilizer:** Feed monthly spring through fall with a balanced house plant fertilizer diluted by half.
- **Propagation:** Seeds or division.

5

Aucuba Japonica

Botanical Name: ***Aucuba japonica*** **'Variegata'**

Green leaves heavily dusted with golden-yellow spots makes Gold Dust Plant a cheery house plant, and a beautiful accent among other foliage plants.

You'll have easy success with this compact, upright shrub because it adapts well to indoor conditions.

In fact, it doesn't need much attention to thrive. It grows well in a pot. Just shade it from direct sunlight, keep it cool and well-watered. Prune it back each spring to keep it small.

Aucuba japonica varieties include both male and female plants that produce clusters of tiny purplish flowers in spring. They're not very attractive, but if pollinated, the flowers are followed by bright red berries carried on the plant through the winter.

- **Prune in spring:** Although slow-growing, Gold Dust Plants will get tall and leggy over time. Prune the stems back hard in spring to keep Japanese aucuba a manageable size indoors and to encourage branching.
- **Pruning tip:** Cut stems at a 45° angle, just above a node (the place where a leaf or branch is attached to the stem). Use sharp pruners to avoid tearing the stems.

- **Repot in spring,** moving up to a container 1 size larger every 2-3 years, or when needed. If your Japanese aucuba is already big, you can top-dress instead by removing the top 2-3 (5-7.5 cm) inches of soil and replace it with fresh potting soil.
- **Clean those beautiful spotted leaves** to keep them dust-free. Wipe them off with a damp cloth.

Plant Care Tips

- **Origin:** Cultivar with parents native to Japan and China
- **Height:** Up to 3 ft (90 cm) indoors. Prune to keep the shrub small.
- **Light:** Bright indirect light. Some cool, direct morning sunlight is fine.
- **Water:** Keep the soil evenly moist from spring through fall. Then, cut back on watering in winter when growth has slowed.
- **Humidity:** Moderate room humidity
- **Temperature:** Cool (45-65°F/7-18°C) temperatures year-round suit this Japanese laurel just fine. In fact, it can tolerate cold — down to 5°F/-15°C — and is sometimes grown as an outdoor shrub.
- **Soil:** Any good potting mix
- **Fertilizer:** Feed monthly spring through fall with a balanced liquid fertilizer diluted by half.
- **Propagation:** Sow seed in spring, Or, take 4 in (10 cm) stem tip cuttings in spring or summer and root in moist potting mix.

6

Baby's Tears

Botanical Name: ***Soleirolia soleirolii***

Baby's Tears gets its name from the tiny, round leaves cascading down slender, fragile stems.

Other common names for this plant include: Mind-Your-Own-Business and Irish Moss.

This fast-growing evergreen has a low, spreading habit that spills beautifully over the sides of a container. Given enough light, it may produce tiny, single flowers in the leaf axils.

Although it seems well-suited for the moist environment of a terrarium, it is invasive and will crowd other plants. I'd recommend putting it in its own pot. Trim with scissors any time to keep it under control.

Repot *S. soleirolii* in spring, when it outgrows its pot.

If you just can't walk past a plant without fussing with it, this one is for you. Water it, mist it, and prune it to your heart's content.

Plant Care Tips

- **Origin:** Italy
- **Height:** Up to 6 in (15 cm)

- **Light:** Will grow in low light, but prefers bright, indirect light. Keep out of direct sun, which will scorch the leaves.
- **Water:** Keep the soil moist at all times. It will not tolerate dry soil.
- **Humidity:** Requires moist air.
- **Temperature:** Normal room temperatures 60-75°F/ 16-24°C
- **Soil:** Any good potting mix
- **Fertilizer:** Feed every 2 weeks spring through summer with balanced liquid house plant fertilizer diluted by half.
- **Propagation:** Divide plant into smaller clumps by gently pulling it apart.

7

Bird Nest Fern

Bird nest fern is a common name applied to several related species of epiphytic ferns in the genus *Asplenium*.

Bird nest fern is one of the easiest types of ferns to grow. This tropical native is fast-growing and will live for many years with good care.

In its natural habitat, it grows as an epiphyte (a plant that grows on trees) in the warm, moist, tropical rain forests. Despite its tropical beginnings, it adapts well to being a house plant. Place your potted fern where it is out of direct sun and away from drafts, which can scorch the fronds. Provide humidity and you'll keep it healthy.

This unique fern grows in the form of a deep rosette of large, shiny, spear-shaped fronds. New fronds unfurl from the centre of the plant. Its fronds are fragile, so I'd put this fern where passersby won't brush up against it.

As Bird Nest Fern ages, the oldest, outer fronds will turn brown. This is normal. You can cut them off at the base to keep the plant looking neat.

Repot young plants in spring, every couple years or when the roots fill the pot. Use a container with drainage holes to avoid overwatering.

This fern's problems are few. Watch for scale insects. If you find an invasion of these pests, spray with soapy water followed by clean water.

Plant Care Tips

- **Origin:** Southeast Asia, Australia
- **Height:** 2 ft (60 cm)
- **Light:** Moderate to bright light. No direct sun. Turn pot regularly for even growth.
- **Water:** Keep soil evenly moist. Water the potting mix, not the centre of the rosette, otherwise it can easily rot. Water less in winter. Yellow fronds are often a sign of overwatering.
- **Humidity:** Moderate. If the relative humidity drops below 50 per cent, use a humidity tray or room humidifier to add moisture to the air around the fern.
- **Temperature:** 60-75°F/16-24°C.
- **Soil:** Peat moss based.
- **Fertilizer:** Feed every 2 weeks in spring and summer with a balanced liquid fertilizer diluted by half.
- **Propagation:** Spores.

8

Boston Fern

Botanical Name: ***Nephrolepsis exaltata***

Boston fern is the most popular of the fern species that originated in Central America and became a fast favourite in parlors and porches in North America during the Victorian era.

Long, arching fronds densely covered with leaflets—called *pinnae*—makes this lush, graceful house plant ideal for a pedestal or a hanging basket.

Today, there are several new cultivars that are getting attention, including 'Fluffy Ruffles' with curly fronds and a dwarf variety 'Timii' that makes an elegant table accent.

Caring for Boston ferns is easy, as long as you meet their need for high humidity. Ferns are native to tropical rainforests, where the relative humidity stays well above 70 per cent. Short of turning your home into a misty rainforest, there are a few things you can do to raise the humidity for your plant.

- **Brown leaflets**—or *pinnae*—are often caused by dry air. Avoid placing your fern near a heat or AC vent because fluctuations in temperature can shock the plant and also cause browning of leaflets. Some browning of frond tips is normal. You can trim brown leaflets with scissors, if you want, to keep it looking neat. Older, lower fronds will naturally turn brown when they die and should be cut off.

- **Fronds that are yellow** and wilted are a sign of overwatering. Reduce amount of water and trim off damaged fronds. Use a container with drainage holes to prevent soggy soil. Check the plant's roots to see if they have rotted. If the roots are mostly black, *get rid of it* — it's too far gone.

Watering Tip

- Always use room-temperature water for your house plants. Cold water shocks these tender tropicals.
- **Repot in spring,** when the roots have filled the container. Move the fern to a pot that's only slightly larger. Want to control its size? Remove the fern from its container and prune off about ¼ of its roots. Then, repot it in the same pot it was in before. This is a good time to divide the fern, if you want.
- **A couple pests** bother this fern. Watch for scale, that look like small, brown discs on leaflets. (Sometimes the brown spores on the undersides of leaflets are mistaken for scale insects. You'll recognize the spores because they appear in two rows under each pinnae.) To remove scale insects, scrape them off with your fingernails. Don't use insecticides on ferns because they are easily damaged by chemicals.

Spider mites are less common, but can cause more damage. Fine webbing between fronds are a sure sign of this destructive pest. Cut off badly affected fronds. Don't use an insecticide, which can damage fronds. If it's warm enough, you can take your fern outdoors to wash it off with tepid water to dislodge these mites. Otherwise, place your fern in the shower.

Misting your fern regularly will prevent an invasion of spider mites that prefer drier conditions. *And, your fern will love the humidity.*

Plant Care Tips

- **Origin:** Central America
- **Height:** Fronds are generally 1-3 ft (30-90 cm) long.
- **Light:** Moderate to bright light. No direct sun. Give the plant a quarter turn every week or so to expose all sides to light.
- **Water:** Keep soil constantly moist, but not soggy. Watch large ferns and hanging basket ferns because they can dry out quickly.
- **Humidity:** High humidity. Use a room humidifier for best results. Misting with room-temperature water helps, if you can mist a few times a day.
- **Temperature:** Normal room temperatures 60-75°F/ 16-24°C.
- **Soil:** Peat moss-based potting mix, such as African violet mix. Or, half-half mixture of peat moss and potting mix.
- **Fertilizer:** Feed every two weeks year-round with a balanced liquid fertilizer diluted by half.
- **Propagation:** Division. You can cut away new plants that grow outside the main root ball and pot them separately. Or, divide a large root ball into smaller clumps with a sharp knife and pot them up.

9

Button Fern

Botanical Name: *Pellaea rotundifolia*

Button fern is a dependable plant that grows well indoors with little care.

Arching fronds densely covered with small, round leaflets makes this New Zealand native an eye-catching accent for any brightly lit room. Place this fern on a table among other house plants or put it in a hanging basket and allow the trail of leathery, button-shaped leaflets to cascade over the side.

Caring for button fern is easy. Unlike most ferns, *Pellaea* tolerates fairly dry conditions. One thing this fern won't tolerate is soggy soil.

Watering Tip

- Allow the top of the soil to dry out slightly before watering again. Fronds that are yellow and wilted are a sign of overwatering. Cut back on water and trim off damaged fronds. Check the plant's roots to see if they have rotted — if they're mostly black, *get rid of it*. It's too far gone.
- Repot in spring, when the roots have filled the pot. Move the fern to a pot that's only slightly larger. Use a pot

with a drainage hole to prevent soggy soil. This is a good time to divide the fern, if you want.

- Keep this evergreen in bright, indirect light and constant room temperature. It won't go dormant. With consistent care, it will grow year-round.

Plant Care Tips

- **Origin:** New Zealand
- **Height:** Up to 1 ft (30 cm)
- **Light:** Bright light, but no direct sun
- **Water:** Water thoroughly, then allow the top 1 in (2.5 cm) of soil to dry out between waterings.
- **Humidity:** Moderate to high humidity.
- **Temperature:** Normal room temperatures 60-75°F/ 16-24°C
- **Soil:** Peat moss based potting mix with added perlite or sand to help drainage.
- **Fertilizer:** Feed monthly year-round with a 20-20-10 liquid fertilizer diluted by half.
- **Propagation:** Division. In spring, divide the plant into 2 or 3 sections with a sharp knife and pot them up. Be sure to get roots with stems attached. Fern spores can be propagated, but germination takes a few months and is not always reliable.

10

Caladium Plant

Botanical Name: *Caladium* hybrids

The paper-thin, heart-shaped leaves of this tropical native are spectacularly decorated, enough to rival even the showiest flowering plant.

Masses of magnificent, 14-inch leaves grow above tall, slender stems. Leaf patterns and colours can vary widely, from white with green veins and borders, to a blush of rose pink, to spotted and marbled red, pink, green, and white. There are hundreds of varieties to choose from—one of the most popular is 'White Queen' shown at bottom.

Caladium 'Thai Beauty', shown at left, is one of the most stunning varieties we've seen. It thrives indoors in indirect light, making this an easy, spectacular accent for your home.

Grow caladiums in summer. These tropical beauties love the warmth and long daylight hours. Plant the tubers in 4-6 inch (10-15 cm) pots, covering with just 1 inch (2.5 cm) of potting mix. Give them a good drink of water, and keep them in a warm spot with indirect light. You can expect those colourful leaves to unfurl within a few weeks.

Caladiums break the rule that all foliage house plants are decorative year-round. This tuberous-rooted hybrid dies down in fall and remains dormant through the winter. That fact — together with the need for high temperatures and high humidity — leads to many of these plants being tossed out after their first growing season.

However, keeping plants till the next year is easy. In the fall, allow the pots to dry out. Cut off the withered leaves, then store the pots at 65-70ºF/18-21ºC in a dark place. Repot the tubers in fresh potting mix in spring and continue with care. Tubers usually can be grown for 2 years before they begin to deteriorate in quality.

Plant Care Tips

- **Origin:** South America
- **Height:** Up to 2 feet (60 cm)
- **Light:** Bright light. Keep out of direct sun because it will cause leaf burn.
- **Water:** Keep potting mix constantly moist throughout the growing season. These plants can drink a lot.
- **Humidity:** Requires moist air. Set the pot on a tray of wet pebbles. Use a room humidifier for best results.
- **Temperature:** Warm 70-85ºF/21-29ºC
- **Soil:** Any good potting mix
- **Fertilizer:** Feed every 2 weeks spring and summer with a high-nitrogen liquid fertilizer diluted by half.
- **Propagation:** Division. When repotting, you can break off small tubers and pot them separately. Plant each tuber in a 4-inch pot about 1-inch deep.

11

California Pitcher Plant

Botanical Name: ***Darlingtonia californica***

California Pitcher Plant is a carnivorous plant that grows in bogs in its native habitat of Northern California and Oregon. Because it is unable to get the nutrients it needs from the soil, it has developed a way to feed from the insects it traps.

The long, tubular green leaves have prominent purple-red veins. They arch at the top, so that the opening faces downward like a hood. Hanging from these hooded tubes are forked leaves that look like serpents' tongues. The upright hooded tubes, together with the "tongues", resemble cobras ready to strike, giving this menacing plant another common name, Cobra Lily.

This carnivorous plant lures insects inside its hooded opening with an intoxicating nectar. Once inside, insects are trapped by tiny hairs that point downward in the tube, making it almost impossible for the prey to escape.

Once you understand its background, you'll understand California Pitcher Plant care. Provide the moist, nutrient-deficient soil and humid air like its natural habitat to keep it healthy. This is one of the few plants researcher knows that doesn't mind cold water. In fact, it prefers a cold drink.

Growing in a bog in the Northwest, it's watered by cold mountain streams and grows best when its roots are cold. If you like, you can water by placing ice cubes (made from distilled or rain water) on top of the soil.

This is a perennial that can be kept from year to year. California Pitcher Plant will go dormant in winter for about 3-4 months. When it dies down, cut off all of the dead pitchers, leaving a few young pitchers. Keep the plant lightly moist and cool during dormancy, with temperatures between 40-45°F/4-7°C. Moving it to a garage or basement for the winter may be ideal . . . just be sure it gets some indirect light and the temperatures don't go below freezing.

New leaves will appear in early spring. You can divide and repot the plant when it starts coming out of dormancy, but be sure to do this before vigorous new growth begins.

Plant Care Tips

- **Origin:** Northern California and Oregon, U.S.A.
- **Height:** Up to 12 in (30 cm)
- **Light:** Bright light, but no direct sun. Fluorescent lighting works well.
- **Water:** Keep soil evenly moist year-round. Because this plant is sensitive to chemicals in tap water, use only distilled or rain water.
- **Humidity:** Moderate to high humidity. Mist the plant every day or set the pot on a tray of wet pebbles.
- **Temperature:** Average room temperatures 60-75°F/16-24°C. In winter, a cold dormancy period is needed 40-45°F/4-7°C
- **Soil:** Use a nutrient-poor medium because rich potting mix will harm its roots. You can plant it in live sphagnum moss, or if that is not available, mix 1 part peat moss with one part perlite or sharp sand.
- **Fertilizer:** Don't fertilize the plant. It makes its own food through photosynthesis when there are no bugs around.
- **Propagation:** Divide in spring when new growth begins. Can be grown from seed, but germination is slow.

12

Cast Iron Plant

Botanical Name: ***Aspidistra elatior***

As its common name suggests, Cast Iron Plant is tough. It will survive low light, infrequent watering and extreme heat that would be deadly to most plants.

In fact, it practically thrives on neglect. Don't overwater—it doesn't like soggy soil. And don't repot it very often—it doesn't like to be disturbed. Respect its Greta Garbo attitude and it will do just fine.

This plant grows slowly in a clump of 6-inch (15 cm) stems with glossy, dark-green leaves growing 24 inches (60 cm) long and 4 inches (10 cm) wide. Small, unattractive, purplish-brown flowers may appear at the plant's base in spring. But, don't expect them. Flowers don't appear often, and they're hardly noticeable.

You can keep its shiny leaves clean by wiping them with a damp cloth. It won't really mind the dust, but you might.

Cast Iron Plant is evergreen and makes a beautiful, easy-care house plant year-round. Best of all, you'll enjoy it for many years.

Plant Care Tips

- **Origin:** China
- **Height:** Up to 3 feet (90 cm).
- **Light:** Moderate to low light. No direct sun. Direct sunlight can cause brown scorched marks on leaves.
- **Water:** In spring and summer, water thoroughly, but allow soil to dry out between waterings. Water less in fall and winter. Yellow leaves are often a sign of overwatering.
- **Humidity:** Average humidity. Will tolerate dry air, but keep plant out of drafts.
- **Temperature:** Adaptable to changing temperatures ranging from 50-85°F/10-29°C.
- **Soil:** Any all-purpose potting mix.
- **Fertilizer:** Feed monthly spring and summer with a balanced liquid fertilizer diluted by half.
- **Propagation:** Divide in spring only when it gets overcrowded in its pot. A slow-grower, it probably won't need divided more often than every 5 years. It's best to remove new shoots (with roots attached) and pot them separately than to repot an old plant.

13

Cat Palm Tree

Botanical Name: ***Chamaedorea cataractarum***

Cat palm tree makes a dramatic house plant and is easy to grow if you give it what it needs.

This lush, tropical palm will thrive in bright light. If you have a sunroom or a sunny window, keep it there. Give your palm a quarter turn once a week so that all sides are exposed to sunlight. A large plant can be placed on a plant caddy to make it easy to move.

Cat palm trees grow in stemless clumps. The pinnate leaves have leaflets that will reach up to 1 ft (30 cm) long and 1 in (2.5 cm) wide. Keep palm fronds clean by gently wiping them with a damp cloth.

This palm needs more moisture than some. Water enough to keep the soil evenly moist, but never soggy. Palms are *not* desert plants as some people believe. Regular watering will help to prevent fronds from turning brown.

- *Brown Leaf Tips* can be caused by dry soil, dry air or tap water that contains fluoride. Increase humidity around the palm, if the air is too dry. Use distilled or rain water to water your palms.

- *Flush Salts:* Palms are sensitive to salts that accumulate in the soil. This build up of soluble salts come from the chemicals in tap water and fertilizers. They can damage foliage and roots. Fortunately, getting rid of excess salts is easy. Place your palm in a sink or take it outdoors on a warm day. Slowly pour tepid water over the potting mix. Allow water to drain out the drainage holes of the pot. Pour more water through the pot, then empty the drainage tray. Flushing salts a couple times a year will make your palm healthier and takes only minutes to do.
- *Repotting your palm* is needed only every 3 years or so. Keeping the roots crowded helps to limit the plant's size, so use a pot that's only 1 size larger than the old pot. Don't pot the palm too deeply—try to keep it at the same depth as it was in the old pot. Also, don't try to spread out those roots. Palm roots are brittle, so keep the root ball intact as much as possible.

Plant Care Tips

- **Origin:** Southern Mexico
- **Height:** Up to 6 ft (1.8 m) indoors
- **Light:** Bright light
- **Water:** Keep soil moist all year long. Put it in a pot with drainage holes to prevent soggy soil. Palms don't like their feet wet.
- **Humidity:** Moderate humidity. If the relative humidity drops below 50 per cent, use a humidity tray or room humidifier. Cat palm also loves to be misted.
- **Temperature:** Average room temperature 60-75°F/ 16-24°C year-round.
- **Soil:** Use a peaty mix that drains well. Mix 1 part sand to 3 parts African violet mix.
- **Fertilizer:** Feed once in spring and again in summer with a time-release fertilizer. I like to use Jobe's Indoor Palm Fertilizer food spikes. It contains the micronutrients that palms need to keep them lush and green.

- **Propagation:** Palms can be grown from seeds, but seeds are slow to germinate and seedlings so slow-growing, you'll wait several years for them to grow into trees. Although Cat palms grow in clumps, researcher wouldn't try to divide them. Cat palm tree roots are fragile and are easily damaged by pulling apart the root ball.

14

China Doll Plant

Botanical Name: ***Radermachera sinica***

China Doll plant is fairly new as a house plant. Introduced to garden centres in the 1980s, it quickly became popular because of its tolerance to the warm, dry air of heated homes.

A small, evergreen shrub, it has long, bipinnate leaves with glossy, deeply veined leaflets that are about 2 in (5 cm) long. Young plants are compact with branching, woody stems. Fast-growing, this plant will quickly become leggy if not pruned back.

Pruning china doll will keep the plant compact and attractive. Cut off as much as you need to in spring and summer.

Pruning tip

Always prune above a leaf node (the place where a leaf is attached to the main stem). Use sharp pruners to avoid tearing the woody stems. Also, pinch off growing tips regularly to encourage the stems to branch out.

In its native habitat of subtropical Southeast Asia, mature plants will produce fragrant, yellow bell-shaped flowers. But plants grown indoors rarely flower.

The keys to success with this China Doll house plant are plenty of bright, indirect light and consistantly moist soil. Yellowing leaves usually mean it has been overwatered. Repot in spring, only when its roots have filled the pot.

Plant Care Tips

- **Origin:** China and Taiwan
- **Height:** Up to 4 ft (1.2 m) indoors
- **Light:** Bright, indirect sunlight
- **Water:** Keep soil evenly moist year-round.
- **Humidity:** Average room humidity.
- **Temperature:** Average room temperatures 60-75°F/ 16-24°C.
- **Soil:** Any good potting mix.
- **Fertilizer:** Feed every 2 weeks spring through fall with 10-10-10 liquid fertilizer diluted by half.
- **Propagation:** Take 4 in (10 cm) stem tip cuttings in spring or summer.

15

Chinese Evergreen

Botanical Name: ***Aglaonema*** **hybrids**

A member of the Aroid family (Araceae), Chinese Evergreen is a hybrid with parents originally from the subtropical forests of Southeast Asia.

A very adaptable plant, it tolerates low light and dry air better than most other house plants. One thing it doesn't like is cold air.

Its large, pointed, dark-green leaves are 6-10 inches (15-25 cm) long, 3 inches (7.5 cm) wide, and heavily marbled with white, cream or silver and white.

As it ages, expect some of the lower leaves to drop off, making it look spindly. Newer varieties of this plant grow in thicker clumps, so mature plants stay compact and bushy. 'Silver Queen' shown here, is a compact variety.

Small flowers may appear in summer, followed by red berries. The berries and sap of this plant are poisonous.

- *Keep it warm*. This plant has no tolerance for the cold. It suffers when exposed to temperatures below 55°F/13°C. Cold air may cause grayish-yellow patches on its leaves. Put your plant in a spot where it won't get cold drafts from doorways or windows.

- *Water regularly*. Consistently moist soil will keep this plant happy. In fact, it can grow in water alone.
- *Don't prune*. All new growth is from the crown of the plant, so don't prune it back or you'll kill it. If it begins to look leggy, plant pothos—or some other low-light plant—in the same container to cover the bare stems.

Plant Care Tips

- **Origin:** Southeast Asia
- **Height:** 2-3 ft (60-90 cm)
- **Light:** Low light. Too much light may cause its leaves to fade.
- **Water:** Keep potting mix evenly moist.
- **Humidity:** Average indoor humidity levels. It will tolerate low humidity. Don't mist, which will cause spots on its leaves.
- **Temperature:** Normal room temperatures 65-75°F/ 18-24°C.
- **Soil:** Any good potting mix.
- **Fertilizer:** From spring through summer, feed monthly with a balanced fertilizer diluted by half.
- **Propagation:** Easy to propagate by stem cuttings or root division. You can root them in water or moist potting mix.

16

Christmas Palm Tree

Botanical Name: ***Veitchia merrillii***

Christmas Palm Tree makes a magnificent tropical house plant.

This adorable palm looks like a miniature of the Royal Palm—the stately giants you see lining boulevards in South Florida and California.

It grows from a single trunk, which supports a crown of arched, pinnate leaves. At the base of the crown, clusters of flowers emerge. In fall, these flowers are replaced with 1 in (2.5 cm) green fruits that ripen to bright red around the end of December. They look like red Christmas lights, giving this stunning tree its common name.

This Southeastern Asia native is surprisingly tolerant of growing in a pot and will thrive indoors as long as it gets plenty of sunshine throughout the year.

You can move this palm outdoors to the patio for the summer, but bring it back inside if the temperature drops near 40ºF. This tropical palm doesn't like the cold at all.

Repot in spring only when the palm becomes severely rootbound. Pots should be deep enough to give roots room to grow. Use a heavy pot — although slow-growing, this palm will eventually get tall and become top-heavy.

Plant Care Tips

- **Origin:** Philippine Islands
- **Height:** Up to 6 ft (1.8 m) indoors
- **Light:** Bright light with some direct sun.
- **Water:** Water regularly, but don't allow soil to get soggy which can cause root rot. Always use a pot with drainage holes.
- **Humidity:** Moderate humidity. If the relative humidity drops below 50 per cent, use a humidity tray or room humidifier.
- **Temperature:** Average room temperature 60-75°F/16-24°C year-round.
- **Soil:** Use a peat moss-based mix that drains well. Mix 1 part sand to 3 parts African violet mix.
- **Fertilizer:** Most indoor plants like a steady diet of liquid plant food, but *not* palms. Palms are slow-growing, especially indoors, and don't need much fertilizer. Feed with a slow-release fertilizer, such as Jobe's Indoor Palm Fertilizer food spikes once in spring and again in summer. It contains the micronutrients that palms need to keep them healthy, lush and green.
- **Propagation:** Christmas Palm Seeds can take months to germinate, so be patient. Sow seeds in spring or summer, covering them lightly with soil. Keep warm (75-80°F/ 24-27°C) and moist.

17

Coffee Plant

Botanical Name: *Coffea arabica*

Coffee plant is the source of the world's most popular breakfast beverage. Not many know, however, that it makes a beautiful and easy-to-grow house plant.

This member of the Rubiaceae family is one of 90 in the *Coffea* genus. It is an evergreen shrub that has glossy, dark-green leaves with ruffled edges on willowy stems.

This coffee bean plant can reach 15 ft or more in its native tropical habitat, but you can cut it back to control its size. Pruning harshly won't hurt it at all.

Pruning tip: Prune coffee plant back in spring to keep it bushy and full. It also gives it an attractive shape. Use clean, sharp pruners to cut the stem at a 45° angle, ¼-inch above a leaf axil (the place where a leaf attaches to the stem).

Repot in spring, moving to a pot 1 size larger. Use a pot with a drainage hole to avoid overwatering.

After 3 or 4 years, *Coffea arabica* produces star-shaped, sweetly scented white flowers. These flowers are followed by green fruits which change to red then to almost black as they ripen, a process that takes several months. Inside each ripened fruit are 2 seeds (or *beans*) that when properly roasted can be ground and made into coffee.

Growing coffee plants indoors is easy. They are vigorous growers and are long-lived. They make attractive house plants, just don't expect them to offer that morning cup of joe. It could take a few years before you see many fruits on it.

Plant Care Tips

- **Origin:** Southern Asia and Tropical Africa.
- **Height:** To 6 ft (1.8 m) indoors.
- **Light:** Bright light, no direct sun.
- **Water:** Keep soil thoroughly moist in spring and summer, barely moist in fall and winter. Provide good drainage.
- **Humidity:** Requires moist air. Use a humidifier for best results.
- **Temperature:** Average room temperatures 60-75°F/ 16-24°C. Not tolerant of freezing temperatures.
- **Soil:** Peat moss based potting mix.
- **Fertilizer:** Feed every 2 weeks spring and summer with a balanced liquid fertilizer diluted by half.
- **Propagation:** Sow fresh seeds in spring. Cuttings are difficult to propagate.

18

Coleus Plant

Botanical Name: ***Coleus blumei*** **(aka** ***Solenostemon scutellarioides*****)**

Coleus plant, also known as Painted Nettle, is often grown outdoors as an annual because it is frost-tender. But it's easy to grow indoors if you can provide bright light.

Distinctive leaf shapes, intricate patterns, and rich colours rival some of the showiest foliage plants.

Boundless varieties of coleus are available. Foliage colours include red, maroon, brown, cream, yellow, orange and green in dramatic combinations and designs.

Leaf edges may be scalloped or ruffled and have a contrasting colour.

Easy-to-grow Coleus 'Rustic Red', shown at left, is available for sale.

- *Pinch your plant.* Coleus plants can get leggy. Pinch growing tips often to encourage them to branch out and stay bushy and full. Also pinch off its small, insignificant flower spikes as soon as you notice them because they will detract from the beautiful foliage.
- *Keep it moist.* Coleus leaves will wilt and may fall off if the soil is too dry. You'll have a much healthier-looking

plant if you keep the soil moist at all times. Use a pot with drainage holes and water thoroughly.

Plant Care Tips

- **Origin**: Southeast Asia
- **Height:** Up to 2 ft (60 cm)
- **Light:** Bright light. Some direct sun is ok, except intense summer sun which will scorch the leaves. Too little light dulls leaf colours and may cause leaves to drop.
- **Water:** Keep soil evenly moist. Leaves will wilt if thirsty.
- **Humidity:** Moderate humidity. Set pot on a tray of wet pebbles.
- **Temperature:** Average room temperatures 60-75°F/ 16-24°C.
- **Soil:** Any good potting mix.
- **Fertilizer:** Feed every 2 weeks spring and summer with a balanced liquid fertilizer diluted by half.
- **Propagation:** Sow coleus seeds in spring. Take 3 in (7 cm) coleus stem tip cuttings in spring or summer. Stem tip cuttings root easily in water or moist soil.

19

Coral Bead Plant

Botanical Name: *Nertera granadensis*

Coral Bead Plant is an unusual-looking ornamental plant that grows in a thick mat of tiny, dark-green leaves on intertwining stems. In early summer, small, white flowers appear followed by orange-red berries. The attractive berries can completely cover the foliage and will last for months.

Because of its need for cool temperatures and humidity, Coral Bead Plant can be somewhat difficult to please indoors. Moving the container outdoors in spring will give it the cool air and bright light it needs to flower and produce berries. Just put the plant in a sheltered spot out of cold winds and direct sun. If the plant is kept very warm, it will be a foliage plant without berries. The plant will still be attractive. In fact, the foliage looks a lot like Baby's Tears (*Soleirolia soleirolii*).

The shallow roots of this plant make it best-suited for a shallow pot. Repot in spring only when needed.

Other common names for this plant are: Bead Plant, Pincushion Plant and Coral Moss.

Plant Care Tips

- **Origin:** New Zealand, Eastern Australia, Southeast Asia and South America

- **Height:** 3 in (8 cm)
- **Light:** Bright light; no direct sun
- **Water:** Keep soil evenly moist
- **Humidity:** Moderate to high humidity. Mist it daily from the time it flowers until the berries have formed.
- **Temperature:** Cool to average 55-65°F/13-18°C.
- **Soil:** Two parts peat moss-based potting mix with 1 part sand or perlite for good aeration
- **Fertilizer:** Feed once a month with a balanced liquid fertilizer diluted by half while the berries are on the plant.
- **Propagation:** Division; gently pull apart clumps and plant them in separate containers. Can be grown from seed or from tip cuttings in spring.

20

Coral Berry

Botanical Name: ***Ardisia crenata***

Clusters of petite flowers followed by bright berries make Coral Berry a delightful house plant.

This evergreen shrub can grow up to 6 ft in its native tropical habitat, but indoors you can expect it to reach about half that height. It's slow-growing, so it'll take a while to get there.

Glossy, deep-green leaves grow to 4 in (10 cm) long and about half as wide. Their serrated edges add to the beauty of this plant.

Tiny white or pale pink flowers grow from the leaf axils on the plant's lower branches in summer. Those slightly aromatic blooms are followed by ¼-in (6 mm) round berries.

Red berries are the real attraction of *Ardisia crenata* and arrive around Christmas time. You'll enjoy the berries on this shrub until it starts flowering again.

Got a reluctant bloomer? Give your plant more humidity and sunlight in spring, when it's starting to form buds. Regular misting with room-temperature water will help increase the moisture in the air around it. Misting also helps to keep away spider mites that prefer dry conditions.

Dropping flower buds are caused by drafty or cold air. Coral Berry likes it cool, but not too cold. It will tolerate a minimum winter temperature of 45°F/7°C.

Prune it back to keep this shrub compact. Pruning each spring before flowering will keep it in shape.

Repot when the roots have filled the pot, moving up to a pot 1 size larger. Wait till late winter to repot—never while it's blooming.

Plant Care Tips

- **Origin:** Southeast Asia
- **Height:** Up to 3 ft (90 cm)
- **Light:** Bright light with some direct sunlight
- **Water:** Keep the soil evenly moist year-round. Never allow it to dry out.
- **Humidity:** Moderate — about 50-60 per cent relative humidity. Stand the pot on a dish of wet pebbles to boost humidity.
- **Temperature:** Cool to average room temperatures 45-65°F/7-18°C.
- **Soil:** Any good potting mix
- **Fertilizer:** Feed every 2 weeks from early spring through summer with a balanced liquid fertilizer diluted by half. In fall and winter, feed monthly.
- **Propagation:** Sow seeds in spring. Or take 4-6 in (10-15 cm) stem tip cuttings in spring and place upright in moist peat moss-based potting mix. Cover the plant and pot in a plastic bag to hold in humidity. Propagating this plant is hit-or-miss. Neither method is easy.

Asparagus densiflorus 'Sprengeri'

Aucuba Japonica 'Variegata'

Soleirolia soleirolii

Baby's Tears

Pilea cadierei

Aluminum Plant in a Pot

Syngonium podophyllum

Arrowhead Plant in a Pot

Pellaea rotundifolia

Caladium Hybrids

Fancy-Leaf Caladium Plant

Darlingtonia californica

Asplenium nidus

Bird Nest Fern

Nephrolepsis exaltata

Boston Fern

Radermachera sinica

Aglaonema Hybrids

Veitchia merrillii

Christmas Palm Tree

California Pitcher Plant

Aspidistra elatior

Cast Iron Plant

Chamaedorea cataractarum

Nertera granadensis

Ardisia crenata

Coral Berry

Calathea sp. 'Corona'

Coffea arabica

Coffee Plant

Coleus blumei

Coleus Plant

21

Corn Plant

Botanical Name: ***Dracaena fragrans*** **'Massangeana'**

Corn plant care is easy. This hardy *Dracaena* is an unbranched, tree-like plant with sword-shaped arching leaves. Its dark-green leaves are 2 ft (60 cm) long and 4 in (10 cm) wide, and have a broad cream-to-yellow stripe down the middle. Strongly scented flowers are occasionally produced on a plant grown in its native habitat, but it rarely flowers indoors.

As it grows, it will shed its lower leaves, leaving a bare stem with a cluster of leaves at its top. New plants may drop a few leaves. This is normal. It needs time to adjust after the shock of being moved to a new home. With your corn plant, care should be taken to keep it away from drafts and direct sun, which can scorch the leaves.

This easy-care house plant will tolerate many abuses, but be careful not to over-water or over-fertilize. Droopy, yellow leaves are a sign it's overwatered and may indicate root rot. Be sure to use a container with a drainage hole and never allow the plant to stand in water.

Prune corn plant back if it grows too tall. If you want, you can propagate the stem tip cuttings for more plants.

Pruning tip: Prune it back in spring or early summer to control its growth. You can cut off the cane at any height. It will sprout a new cluster of leaves from where it was cut.

Repot in spring only when the plant's roots have filled the container. It is slow-growing and likely won't need repotted more than every 3 years. Corn plant prefers to be slightly root-bound, so keep it in a smallish container—a heavy container will prevent it from toppling because this plant can get top-heavy.

Good indoor corn plant care will allow you to enjoy your plant for many years—it's a long-lived house plant.

Plant Care Tips

- **Origin:** Tropical East Africa
- **Height:** Grows slowly but can reach 6 ft (1.8 m)
- **Light:** Bright light. Will tolerate low light.
- **Water:** Spring through fall, keep the soil moist, but not soggy. In winter, allow top 2 in (5 cm) of soil to dry out between waterings.
- **Humidity:** Average to moderate humidity.
- **Temperature:** Average room temperatures 60-75°F/ 16-24°C work fine for corn plant. Care should be taken that it isn't exposed to temperatures below 55°F/13°C.
- **Soil:** Any good potting mix that drains well.
- **Fertilizer:** Feed monthly spring through fall with a balanced liquid fertilizer diluted by half.
- **Propagation:** Take 4-6 inch (10-15 cm) stem tip cuttings in spring or summer and pot them in moist potting mix.

22

Corona Prayer Plant

Botanical Name: *Calathea* sp. 'Corona'

Corona Prayer Plant deserves its place among the showy plants of the Maranta (Marantaceae) family.

Its broad, silvery-green leaves taper to a point and are edged with a wide band of dark green. New leaves are curled as they emerge, showing their purplish red undersides. And like its family members, this tropical foliage plant folds its leaves at night as hands in prayer.

The secret to keeping it happy is to provide high humidity. Do anything you can to keep the relative humidity above 60 per cent. Place it on a humidity tray or use a room humidifier. Calatheas also love to be misted with rainwater. Raising the humidity will keep away the spider mites that are attracted to this plant.

Display Ideas: Group calatheas with other humidity-loving plants, such as bromeliads and ferns. Or show off a single plant by placing it on a pedestal plant stand by itself.

Repot calathea in spring to give it fresh potting mix. Need a new container? Check out stylish, new house plant pots here.

Plant Care Tips

- **Origin:** Central America and Brazil
- **Height:** Up to 18 in (45 cm)
- **Light:** Moderate to bright light. No direct sun.
- **Water:** Keep soil evenly moist. Do not allow the soil to get soggy. Use distilled water or rainwater because this plant is sensitive to fluoride and salts in tap water.
- **Humidity:** Moderate to high humidity.
- **Temperature:** Average to warm 65-85°F/18-29°C.
- **Soil:** Any good potting mix that drains well.
- **Fertilizer:** Feed every 2 weeks spring and summer with a 10-10-5 liquid fertilizer diluted by half. In fall and winter, feed monthly.
- **Propagation:** Division. Divide rhizomes of mature plants in spring or early summer.

23

Creeping Fig or Climbing Fig

Botanical Name: ***Ficus pumila***

Creeping fig has small, heart-shaped leaves that densely cover its long stems. Its growing habits make it a versatile plant indoors. To show off its thickly leafed vines, put this trailing, climbing, creeping ficus plant in a hanging basket.

Better yet, you can train its aerial roots to sink into a moss support, trellis or topiary. Tie it loosely to a support with florist's wire and this climbing fig will readily take hold.

Want another option? Plant it as a ground cover beneath a tall house plant and allow the stems to spill over the sides of the container. It makes a nice complement to Norfolk Island pine or a braided weeping fig (*F. benjamina*).

Plant Care Tips

- **Origin:** China, Japan
- **Height:** Trailing to 3 ft (90 cm)
- **Light:** Bright light. Will tolerate low light, but not direct sun. Dry, shriveled leaves are caused by too much sun.
- **Water:** Keep soil lightly moist spring through fall. Water less in winter.
- **Humidity:** Moderate to high room humidity.

- **Temperature:** Will tolerate cool to warm temperatures (55-85°F/13-29°C)
- **Soil:** Any good potting mix.
- **Fertilizer:** Feed monthly spring through fall with a balanced liquid fertilizer diluted by half.
- **Propagation:** Take stem cuttings in spring and root in fresh potting mix.
- **Don't overwater.** Water thoroughly when potting mix is dry 1 inch down. Reduce water in the winter when growth has slowed.
- **Prune it back.** This plant is fast-growing and needs some help from you to shape it or train it. Prune off new stems regularly to encourage branching and to shape them as they grow. Pruning up to one-third in spring will keep the plant compact.
- **Repot in spring.** This creeping ficus houseplant prefers to be slightly pot-bound. Repot every 3 years, moving to a pot 1 size larger or keep it in the same pot and just give it fresh potting mix.

24

Croton Plants

Botanical Name: ***Codiaeum variegatum pictum***

Croton plants stiff, leathery leaves in bold colours of yellow, pink, red, orange and green make it a beautiful and popular house plant. Another common name for croton plant is Joseph's Coat.

Crotons are not easy to please. The keys to success are plenty of sunshine, a warm, draft-free environment, moist soil, and humid air. Dry air and soil will cause croton leaves to fall off.

- *Too tall? Top them*. The plants are naturally bushy, so they shouldn't need pruning. If they get too big, you can cut them back in spring and propagate the stem cuttings.
- *To repot...or not?* Repot in spring, moving to a pot only 1 size larger. You can control croton plant's size by keeping it in the same container, so that its roots are confined. When the plant reaches the size you want, top-dress annually instead.
- *Give them space*. If you bought a container that has 2 or 3 plants in it (which is fairly common), keep them together for the first year. The next year, give them the space they

need by separating them. Separate the plants by carefully cutting through their roots with a serrated knife, then pot them in their own containers.

Are croton plants poisonous? Oh, yes. A member of the Euphorbia family, this plant has poisonous sap. Don't be afraid of crotons, but take some precautions. Keep croton away from children and pets and wear gloves while handling it.

Plant Care Tips

- **Origin:** Pacific Islands, Malaysia, Northern Australia
- **Height:** To 3 ft (90 cm)
- **Light:** Bright light and at least 3 hours of direct sun each day.
- **Water:** Keep soil mix evenly moist with tepid water.
- **Humidity:** High humidity. Mist daily if possible. Stand the plant on a tray of wet pebbles.
- **Temperature:** Warm 65-85°F, 18-29°C
- **Soil:** Peat moss based potting mix.
- **Fertilizer:** Feed every 2 weeks from early spring through summer with a balanced liquid fertilizer diluted by half.
- **Propagation:** Take stem cuttings in spring and dip in rooting hormone before inserting in a half-half mix of sand and peat moss. Croton cuttings root in about a month.

25

Dragon Tree

Botanical Name: ***Dracaena marginata***

Madagascar Dragon Tree is a bold accent if you have the space. It starts out as a thick tuft of spiky leaves. As it grows, the lower leaves naturally fall, leaving a cluster of dramatic, spear-shaped leaves above a bare woody stem. Its narrow, red-edged leaves can grow about 12-16 in (30-40 cm) long.

This exotic house plant is slow-growing, but will reach 6 ft (1.8 m) tall indoors. You can control its height by simply cutting off the top.

- *Pruning tip:* Prune it back in spring or early summer to control its growth. You can cut off the cane at any height. Within weeks, it will sprout a new cluster of leaves from where it was cut.
- *Dracaena* care is easy. Dragon Tree thrives in average room conditions, tolerating dry winter air and low light levels that are deadly to most plants. This dynamic house plant also handles changing temperatures and humidity levels. Just don't overwater. It will not tolerate soggy soil, which can cause root rot.

It even shrugs off pests, although dry air may attract spider mites to its leaves. Regular misting with water will do double-duty, raising the humidity and keeping those pests away.

Plant Care Tips

- **Origin:** Madagascar
- **Height:** To 6 ft (1.8 m)
- **Light:** Bright light. Avoid direct sunlight in summer.
- **Water:** Keep soil lightly moist spring through fall, slightly drier in winter. Do not let soil get waterlogged.
- **Humidity:** Average room humidity. Will tolerate dry air.
- **Temperature:** Normal room temperatures. 60-75°F/16-24°C
- **Soil:** Any good potting mix.
- **Fertilizer:** Feed every 2 weeks in spring and summer with a 10-10-10 liquid fertilizer diluted by half.
- **Propagation:** Cut off the cane at any height and root them like stem cuttings.

26

Dumb Cane

Botanical Name: ***Dieffenbachia***

Dumb Cane get its name from its poisonous sap that causes painful swelling of the mouth and throat, as well as vocal loss if eaten. It also can cause skin irritation, so researcher recommends wearing gloves while handling this plant.

This attractive and popular house plant features a single, thick trunk that unwinds into several trunks as it matures. Its handsome, broad leaves are about 10 inches (25 cm) long and are splashed, streaked or speckled in green and white.

Pruning Tip: Cut back your dieffenbachia if it grows too tall. Use sharp pruners to cut off the top of the plant, leaving a few leaves. New growth will sprout from where it was cut.

Any problems with Dumb Cane will show in its leaves.

- The older leaves may turn yellow and drop off. This is normal. If new leaves fall off, the plant is too cold. Keep it away from doorways or windows where could be exposed to cold drafts.
- *Brown leaf tips* are caused by sporadic watering. Water regularly, but don't allow the soil to get soggy.
- *Curled, crispy leaf tips* could indicate too much fertilizer. Flush soil with clean water to wash away any accumulated fertilizer. Wait a month before feeding again.

- If they are not getting enough light, leaves lose their variegation. Give the plant moderate to bright light, but not direct sun.
- *Scorched leaves* (dry, brown spots) are caused by strong, direct sunlight.

Repot in spring or early summer when the plant has outgrown its pot. Always use a container with drainage holes to prevent soggy soil.

Although this plant is native to the South American rain forests, it tolerates average room humidity quite well and is easy to grow.

Plant Care Tips

- **Origin:** Brazil
- **Height:** 1-6 ft (30 cm - 1.8 m) Newer hybrids are more compact reaching only 1-2 ft (30-60 cm)
- **Light:** Bright light, no direct sun. Turn plant often to encourage even growth.
- **Water:** Water thoroughly and allow soil to dry out a bit between waterings.
- **Humidity:** Average room humidity.
- **Temperature:** Normal room temperatures 65-75°F/ 18-24°C.
- **Soil:** Soilless potting mix to allow good drainage.
- **Fertilizer:** Feed spring through summer every 2 weeks with a liquid fertilizer diluted by half. In fall and winter, feed monthly.
- **Propagation:** Take 3-5 inch (8-13 cm) stem tip cuttings in spring or early summer and insert in moist potting mix. Pups that emerge from the base of the plant can be cut away and planted in their own containers.

27

Elephant's Ear

Botanical Name: ***Alocasia x amazonica***

Elephant's Ear is an exotic house plant with striking foliage. Thick, upright stems carry arrow-shaped leaves with scalloped edges. The bold silver-green veins make a dramatic pattern on glossy, dark-green leaves.

Just like other members of the Aracae family, its flowers are composed of a spadix surrounded by a spathe. On this plant, however, they are insignificant. It's the spectacular foliage that makes it well worth growing.

Caring for Elephant's Ear

This tropical house plant can be somewhat fussy, prefering the high humidity of a greenhouse to an average home. However, a room humidifier and frequent misting of the leaves will give it the moist air it craves. Regular misting also helps to keep away red spider mites that like to attack this plant.

Repot in spring when necessary. Use a container with drainage holes to prevent root rot.

Give it a rest period in winter, allowing the soil to become almost dry between waterings and stop fertilizing.

It may go dormant if it dries out completely. But don't give up on it — it'll recuperate in a month or two with good care. Continue to provide plenty of humidity with a pebble tray or misting every day.

Plant Care Tips

- **Origin:** Tropical Asia
- **Height:** To 2 ft (60 cm)
- **Light:** Bright light, but no direct sun.
- **Water:** Keep soil moist spring through fall when plant is actively growing. Water sparingly in winter, allowing soil to become almost dry between waterings.
- **Humidity:** Requires moist air. Use a room humidifier for best results.
- **Temperature:** Average to warm 65-75°F/18-24°C
- **Soil:** Peat moss based potting mix.
- **Fertilizer:** Feed every 2 weeks spring through fall with a 20-10-10 liquid fertilizer diluted by half. Do not feed in winter.
- **Propagation:** Division. Divide rhizomes in spring and pot in separate containers. Keep the top surface of the rhizome above the soil line so that the growing stems don't rot at soil level.

28

English Ivy Plant Care

Botanical Name: ***Hedera helix***

With lobed leaves and lush, trailing vines, English Ivy is a beautiful accent plant.

This ivy is a vigorous grower with strong, wiry stems densely covered with distinctive foliage. Although commonly grown as a hanging plant indoors, its aerial roots can easily be trained to climb a moss stick or trellis.

There are hundreds of types of ivy varieties — some with plain green leaves, others are variegated with yellow, gold or creamy white.

Tips for Growing English Ivy House Plants

Cool, moist air and evenly moist soil will help your English Ivy thrive indoors. Protect it from drafts. Mist the plant often to keep its leaves from drying out. Misting also helps to keep away spider mites that love to attack this plant.

Growing ivy with plenty of bright light will help variegated ivies to keep their colour. Prune off any stems of variegated ivy that reverts to all green.

Caution: The leaves of this plant are poisonous if eaten and it can cause skin irritation. It's a good idea to wear gloves while handling this plant.

Plant Care Tips

- **Origin:** Europe
- **Height:** It will climb as high as it is allowed to.
- **Light:** Bright light, but no direct sun. It thrives under fluorescent light. If variegated varieties change to mostly green, it isn't getting enough light.
- **Water:** Keep soil evenly moist but not soggy spring through fall; slightly drier in winter.
- **Humidity:** Increase the humidity by misting with water or standing the plant on a tray of wet pebbles.
- **Temperature:** Cool to average room temperatures 50-70°F/10-21°C.
- **Soil:** Soilless potting mix or any that provides good drainage.
- **Fertilizer:** Feed monthly from spring through fall with a high-nitrogen liquid fertilizer.
- **Propagation:** Take 3-4 in (8-10 cm) stem tip cuttings in spring and root in moist soil or water.

29

European Fan Palm Tree

Botanical Name: ***Chamaerops humilis***

European Fan Palm (aka Mediterranean Fan Palm) is the only palm native to Europe, and is hardier than most palms. Give it the warm, sunny days and cool nights of its native dry mountain habitat and you'll find that it's easy to grow.

This shruby palm will eventually reach about 4 ft (1.2 m) tall indoors. As the plant matures, the trunk develops numerous sharp spines.

Fine-textured fronds grow in a rounded fan of 10-20 leaflets that reach up to 24 in/60 cm wide. The leaflets range in colour from silvery green to blue-green and naturally split as they mature.

Repot only when needed. This palm has fragile roots, so repot only every 3 years or so. They grow deep — so keep this palm in a deep pot.

Once the plant reaches the size you want, you can top-dress it instead by replacing the top couple inches of potting mix. Take care not to disturb any roots that may be near the surface.

Watering tip: Palms are sensitive to chlorine, fluoride, and other chemicals often found in tap water, as well as the salt in softened water. Use only distilled or filtered water to avoid the build-up of chemicals.

Although slow-growing, it is well worth the wait because even small plants will stand out, making it a stunning sculptural accent for the home. This fan palm tree is also long-lived, so you'll enjoy it for many years.

Plant Care Tips

- **Origin:** Mediterranean region of Southwestern Europe (Spain, Portugal, France, Italy and Malta)
- **Height:** 4 ft (1.2 m) tall.
- **Light:** Needs at least 4 hours of direct sun a day.
- **Water:** Keep constantly moist in spring and summer. In fall and winter, allow top 2 in (5 cm) of soil to dry out between waterings.
- **Humidity:** Average room humidity.
- **Temperature:** 70-80°F/21-27°C days; 50-60°F/10-16°C nights.
- **Soil:** Mix two parts peat moss-based potting mix and one part sharp sand. Repot only when necessary, about every three years.
- **Fertilizer:** Feed monthly spring and summer with a balanced liquid fertilizer diluted by half. Do not feed in fall and winter.
- **Propagation:** Sow seeds in spring, barely covering the seeds with soil. Keep them warm (75-80°F/24-27°C) and moist. Palm seeds can take several weeks to germinate, so be patient. European palm is one of the few palms that readily produces suckers that can be cut away and potted in their own containers.

30

False Aralia

Botanical Name: ***Dizygotheca elegantissima.***

False Aralia has slender leaflets that grow in a circle at the tops of stems so that they look like fingers, giving this house plant another common name: Finger Aralia.

New coppery brown foliage turns a dark, blackish-green as the plant matures. Its narrow, serrated leaflets give this small tree a lacy appearance, making it a graceful addition to a collection of tropical house plants.

- **Leaf drop:** *Dizygotheca* likes to stay put. Moving it to a new location may cause its leaves to drop. Shedding leaves may also indicate that humidity is too low. Mist the plant every morning or stand the pot on a tray of wet pebbles. Misting also helps to prevent spider mites that may invade this plant.
- **Pruning:** False Aralia is slow-growing and doesn't need pruned unless you want to control its height. Over time, it will drop its lower leaves, revealing a single tree-like trunk. If you want, you can keep it short and shrubby by cutting it back each year. Don't be afraid to prune it to 6 inches (15 cm) from the soil level. Spring is the best time to cut it back. New offsets will grow from the base of the plant.

- **Repotting:** Repot in spring only when it has outgrown its pot, but use the smallest container that will hold its roots. It grows best when its roots are confined. Taller plants should be potted in a heavy container to prevent toppling.

Plant Care Tips

- **Origin:** South Pacific.
- **Height:** This Pacific Island native can grow to 20 ft (6 m) in the wild, but indoors this tree will slowly reach about 6 ft (1.8 m).
- **Light:** Bright light, no direct sun.
- **Water:** Water thoroughly and allow top 1 in (2.5 cm) of soil to dry out between waterings. Wilted leaves are a sign of overwatering.
- **Humidity:** Moderate to high humidity.
- **Temperature:** Warm 65-85°F/18-29°C. Do not expose it to temperatures below 60°, which can cause leaf drop.
- **Soil:** Any good potting mix.
- **Fertilizer:** Feed every two weeks with a balanced liquid fertilizer (such as 10-10-10) diluted by half. In fall and winter, feed monthly.
- **Propagation:** Seeds or stem tip cuttings. Take stem tip cuttings in spring. For best results, dip cut end in hormone rooting powder before inserting in moist potting mix. Cover with a plastic bag to raise the humidity around the cutting. Keep it warm and out of direct sunlight.

31

Fibre Optic Grass

Botanical Name: *Isolepis cernua* aka *Scirpus cernuus*

Fibre Optic Grass is a fountain-like ornamental grass with small, silvery white flowers at the tips. Its resemblance to fibre optic wire lends its common names, including Live Wire Grass.

If you like unusual indoor plants, you'll want to add this ornamental sedge to your collection.

Growing in a clumping mound, it spills over the sides of a container as it grows, making it ideal for a tall planter or even a hanging pot. Eye-catching on its own, this decorative grass also adds texture among a display of foliage and flowering plants.

Perennial and evergreen, this showy grass is an easy-care house plant. Keep it warm and moist, give it sunlight, and you can expect blooms from spring through fall.

Plant Care Tips

- **Water generously:** Don't allow the soil to dry out. Foliage will turn yellow then brown when it gets too dry. Water thoroughly and often to keep the soil *at least* evenly moist at all times. Fibre Optic Grass is native to marsh areas, so it doesn't mind soggy soil.

- **Repot in spring**, moving up to a container 1 size larger every 2-3 years, or when it becomes crowded. Spring is also a good time to divide the plant, if you want.
- **Origin:** Southern Europe and Northern Africa
- **Height:** Up to 1 ft (30 cm)
- **Light:** Bright light to full sun
- **Water:** Keep the soil moist or wet at all times. Native to marshlands, this is one plant you can't overwater.
- **Humidity:** Moderate room humidity
- **Temperature:** Average to warm room temperatures (65-80°F/18-27°C) year-round. If you put this tender ornamental out on the patio for the summer, bring it back in when the temperature drops. It won't tolerate frost.
- **Soil:** Peat moss-based potting mix
- **Fertilizer:** Feed monthly spring through fall with a balanced liquid fertilizer diluted by half.
- **Propagation:** Sow seed in spring, barely covering the seeds. Keep the soil warm (around 70°F/21°C) and constantly moist. Mature plants can be divided and potted separately.

32

Ficus Alii

Botanical Name: *Ficus binnendiijkii* 'Alii'

Ficus Alii doesn't exist in the wild. 'Alii' is a fairly new cultivar and makes a beautiful indoor tree.

The long, narrow leaves are naturally glossy and taper to a point. As this ficus tree grows, it may drop its lower leaves revealing a bare woody trunk, giving this tree a palm-like appearance. Sometimes its trunks are braided by growers making it look like a topiary.

Its care is easier than many of its relatives. You'll find it's less tempermental than *F. benjamina*, that drops its leaves when it doesn't get what it wants. However, leaf drop is possible with 'Alii' if it doesn't get enough light and regular waterings.

Repot only when necessary in spring, using the smallest pot that will contain its roots. Ficus plants are slow-growing and prefer to be slightly pot-bound. Use a pot with drainage holes to prevent overwatering.

Ficus Alii seems resistant to pests. However, watch for whiteflies and scale insects that tend to bother ficus plants. Treat any infestation immediately.

Plant Care Tips

- **Origin:** Hybrid

- **Height:** Up to 10 ft (3 m) indoors. Pruning ficus will control its size.
- **Light:** Bright, indirect light year-round.
- **Water:** Water soil thoroughly, then allow top 1 in (2.5 cm) to dry out between waterings. Use lukewarm water because cold water may cause leaf loss. Avoid using softened water—it contains salts which can harm ficus plants.
- **Humidity:** Average room humidity.
- **Temperature:** Average room temperatures 60-75°F/ 16-24°C.
- **Soil:** Any good potting mix.
- **Fertilizer:** Feed every two weeks spring through fall with a balanced liquid fertilizer diluted by half.
- **Propagation:** Stem tip cuttings and air layering. Propagating ficus trees is not easy for the amateur to do at home. These trees are slow to root from either method.

33

Fiddle Leaf Fig

Botanical Name: ***Ficus lyrata***

Enormous leaves shaped like violins make Fiddle Leaf Fig a dramatic accent.

In its native habitat, this fig tree from the Moraceae family will reach 40 ft (12 m) tall. Fortunately, it grows very slowly and stays much shorter when grown indoors.

Controlling its height is easy to do. Prune off the top of young plants to promote branching and to control its growth. You can also control its size by keeping it in a small container.

Repot only when necessary in spring, using the smallest pot that will contain its roots. Use a heavy container to keep it from toppling over. This plant can get top-heavy.

Its bold, prominently veined leaves grow to 12 in (30 cm) long and 6 in (15 cm) wide with wavy edges. Keep the naturally glossy leaves clean by wiping them often with a damp cloth. This tropical native also loves to be misted.

Fiddle Leaf Fig tree produces edible fruit in the wild, but rarely when grown indoors.

Plant Care Tips

- **Origin:** Western Africa

- **Height:** 3-10 ft (90 cm - 3 m) indoors
- **Light:** Bright light
- **Water:** Keep soil evenly moist. Drooping yellow leaves are a sign of overwatering.
- **Humidity:** Average room humidity.
- **Temperature:** Average room temperatures 60-75°F/ 16-24°C.
- **Soil:** Any good potting mix.
- **Fertilizer:** Feed 3 times a year during the growing season (spring-summer-fall) with a balanced liquid fertilizer diluted by half.
- **Propagation:** Stem tip cuttings and air layering. Propagating large-leaf fig trees is not easy for the amateur to do at home. These trees are slow to root from either method.

34

Fishtail Palm Tree

Botanical Name: ***Caryota mitis***

Fishtail Palm gets its common name from the ragged-edged, ribbed texture of the dark-green leaflets that grow on upright stems. Its triangular leaflets are unique, and over time naturally split at the ends—just like a fish tail.

Caryota mitis grows in a clump, with several stems rising from its base that can easily be divided.

I don't sell palms directly from this site, but I highly recommend Real Palm Trees.

They offer two sizes of this Fishtail Palm Tree, plus a variety of other small palms that are suitable for growing indoors. You can expect top-quality palms and excellent service. Best of all, your satisfaction is guaranteed with your purchase. You don't have to worry about ordering from this company.

Fishtail Palm tree is native to Southeast Asia, where it thrives in the warm temperatures and humidity of its tropical habitat.

This tropical palm is one of the easiest indoor palm plants to grow, requiring little care.

Tips

Add a little sand to the potting soil to speed up drainage. Use a ratio of 3:1 potting mix to sand. Use horticultural sand, not the type from the beach, which contains salts and impurities that can damage palms.

It is more tolerant of drier soil than overwatering. Put it in a container with a drainage hole. Water thoroughly then allow the soil to dry slightly between waterings.

Repot only when roots grow out of the bottom of the drainage hole. This palm prefers to be slightly pot-bound.

Brown leaf tips are likely caused by dry soil or — more likely — dry air. Use any practical means to increase the humidity around this palm. A room humidifier works best.

Do not prune palm trees unless an old branch dies. Palm trees grow from the tip of the branch. If you prune or pinch off the newest frond where it is attached to the stem, it will stop all new growth.

Grown as an indoor palm tree, it can reach 6 ft (1.8 m) indoors, therefore it needs some vertical space. This tree becomes more lush and attractive as it matures.

Plant Care Tips

- **Origin:** Burma, Malaysia
- **Height:** Up to 6 ft (1.8 m)
- **Light:** Bright light
- **Water:** Water thoroughly then allow soil to dry slightly between waterings. Water less in winter when growth has slowed. Use filtered or distilled water because tap water may contain fluoride, chlorine and other chemicals that can damage palms.
- **Humidity:** Average to moderate. If relative humidity drops below 50 per cent, stand the pot on a humidity tray or use a room humidifier.
- **Temperature:** Average to warm temperatures 65-85°F/ 18-29°C

- **Soil:** Any good potting mix. Adding sand to the mix will help speed up drainage.
- **Fertilizer:** Feed once in early summer with slow-release fertilizer. I like to use Jobe's Indoor Palm Fertilizer food spikes. It contains the micronutrients that palms need to keep them lush and green.
- **Propagation:** Sow seeds in spring or summer, keeping the soil warm and moist. Offsets can be carefully cut away from the plant and potted in separate containers.

35

Foxtail Fern

Botanical Name: ***Asparagus densiflorus*** **'Myers'**

Upright, emerald plumes make foxtail fern a gorgeous accent plant for container groupings or staging among tropicals.

This beautiful fern is easy to grow and, some say, more decorative than its close relative, the asparagus fern.

Fronds densely covered with 1 in (2.5 cm) needle-like leaflets give this fern a delicate, feathery appearance. But, don't let its delicate appearance fool you. In its native, warm temperature forests of Africa, this fern is an aggressive grower and can be invasive. It's not a problem, though, contained in a pot. Cut it back or divide it in spring to keep it under control.

- **Prune it back.** Cut back stems to keep this fern compact and bushy. Trim off old, faded fronds to make room for new growth and to keep the plant looking its best.
- **Repot in spring.** Move to a pot only 1 size larger. Allow 1-2 in (2.5-5 cm) space from the rim of the pot, because the fleshy, tuberous roots sometimes force the potting mix up as they grow.
- **Leaf drop** is usually a symptom of too much sunlight — or, more likely — dry soil. Foxtail fern likes dappled

sunlight. Water regularly, but take care not to overwater. The plant's thick, tuberous roots store water and soggy soil can cause root rot. Raising the humidity can help.

Plant Care Tips

- **Origin:** South Africa
- **Height:** Up to 3 ft (90 cm) long
- **Light:** Bright light
- **Water:** Water thoroughly, allowing soil to dry out a little between waterings. Too much water can lead to root rot. Water sparingly in winter, but do not allow soil to dry out completely.
- **Humidity:** Prefers moist air. Set pot on a tray of wet pebbles and mist leaves with room- temperature water.
- **Temperature:** Average room temperatures 60-75°F/ 16-24°C.
- **Soil:** Any good potting mix.
- **Fertilizer:** Feed monthly spring through fall with a balanced house plant fertilizer diluted by half.
- **Propagation:** Division. Divide overcrowded plants in spring. Remove the plant from its pot and cut through the thick roots with a sharp knife to avoid pulling and tearing them.

36

Friendship Plant

Botanical Name: ***Pilea involucrata*** **'Moon Valley'**

Friendship Plant has quilted leaves of apple green with deep bronze veins that make it a joy to grow indoors.

This is a bushy, fast-growing plant with ovate leaves that grow in opposite pairs. Pinch off growing tips, if you want, to keep the plant compact. Those cuttings will root easily, so don't toss them out. Share them with friends or pot them up for more plants.

'Moon Valley' has a more upright habit than the species, which is a trailing plant. Its toothed, deeply textured leaves feature dark-red undersides. Clusters of tiny, pink-green flowers may appear in spring, but they are insignificant compared to the showy foliage.

Place Friendship Plant near a window, but away from direct sunlight, which can scorch its leaves. Also keep it away from heat vents or drafty windows.

- *Humidity tip:* High humidity is a must. It's a good idea to use a pebble tray or room humidifier for Friendship Plant. It makes an excellent terrarium plant.
- Dropped leaves can be caused by either dry or soggy soil. However, you can expect the lower leaves to fall off

as plants get older, making them look leggy and unattractive. That's another good reason to propagate stem cuttings for more plants — you may want to replace your plant after a few years.

Plant Care Tips

- **Origin:** Central and South America
- **Height:** Up to 12 in (30 cm)
- **Light:** Moderate to bright light; no direct sunlight
- **Water:** Keep soil evenly moist spring through fall; slightly drier in winter.
- **Humidity:** High humidity. If relative humidity drops below 50 per cent, place pot on a tray of wet pebbles or use a room humidifier.
- **Temperature:** Average to warm room temperatures (65-80°F/18-27°C) suit this tropical plant.
- **Soil:** Peat moss-based mix or African violet mix.
- **Fertilizer:** Feed monthly in spring and summer with a balanced liquid fertilizer diluted by half.
- **Propagation:** Take stem tip cuttings in spring. Put the stem in moist potting mix, then firm the mix around the stem so that it stands up. Enclose the whole pot in a plastic bag to hold in humidity. Cuttings root easily.

37

Grape Ivy Plant

Botanical Name: ***Cissus rhombifolia***

Grape Ivy is a vigorous, evergreen vine with handsome, glossy compound leaves, each bearing 3 leaflets. Young leaves are fuzzy, giving them a silvery sheen. It's extremely adaptable to indoor conditions and makes an easy house plant.

Pot ivy in a hanging basket to show off its beautiful trailing foliage. Large ivy plants can be trained up a trellis or moss pole. Its sturdy vines will scramble up any support, climbing and clinging with its curling tendrils.

- *Pinch and prune*. Growing tips are tender and can be pinched off with your fingernails. Regular pinching will keep your grape ivy plant compact and bushy. *Don't toss out those stem tips* either. You can propagate them for more plants.
- Control the plant's size by pruning every spring. Always cut at a 45° angle above a leaf node (the place where a leaf attaches to the stem). If a lower stem becomes bare, don't be afraid to cut it back at the base.
- *Repot in spring* every couple years or when roots fill the pot. Use one with drainage holes to prevent soggy soil and root rot.

- Grape ivy doesn't go dormant in the winter, but growth slows down. One of the common problems with ivy plant care is overwatering. Allow soil to dry out a bit between waterings in winter and stop fertilizing until spring.

Plant Care Tips

- **Origin:** South America
- **Height:** Size varies with variety. Some plants will climb up to 6 ft (1.8 m) or more with support. You can keep it to 2 ft (60 cm) with pruning. Grape ivy bonsai tree stays small.
- **Light:** Moderate to bright light. Protect your plant from direct sun, which can cause brown scorch marks on the leaves.
- **Water:** Water generously throughout the growing season, keeping the soil evenly moist. Water less in winter, allowing the top 1 inch (2.5 cm) of soil to dry between waterings.
- **Humidity:** Grape ivies like relative humidity near 40-60 per cent. Brown leaf tips are sometimes caused by dry air. Misting can help, but give your ivy plant good air circulation to prevent powdery mildew.
- **Temperature:** Warm in spring and summer (65-80°F/ 18-27°C). Slightly cooler in fall and winter (50-70°F/ 10-21°C).
- **Soil:** Peat moss-based potting mix or African violet mix.
- **Fertilizer:** Feed monthly in spring and summer with a balanced liquid fertilizer diluted by half.
- **Propagation:** Take 3-4 in (7.5-10 cm) stem tip cuttings in late spring. Strip off the lower leaves and dip cut ends in rooting hormone powder. Then insert cuttings in a 1:1 mixture of moist peat and perlite. Enclose the pot in a plastic bag to maintain humidity. Roots should grow in 6-8 weeks.

38

Heartleaf Philodendron

Botanical Name: ***Philodendron scandens***

Heartleaf philodendron is a popular house plant because it is extremely easy to grow. It's also known as the Sweetheart Plant.

Heart-shaped, glossy leaves emerge bronze, then quickly turn green. The leaves are typically 2-4 in (5-10 cm) long, and cover its long, slender stems that can grow to 4 ft (1.2 m) or more.

Pinch your Plant

- Without pinching, it will grow with long, single stems and become lanky. You can pinch it back anytime to help it branch out, keeping the plant bushy and full. Always pinch above a leaf node (the place where a leaf is attached to the stem). A new stem will grow from that node.

Pinching Tips

- Try to pinch close to the node because any bare stem that is left will die, and the node will not grow a new stem. Make a clean cut — you want to avoid jagged tears, which can attract disease. You can use your fingernails to pinch, or use sharp scissors or pruners.

Or, let it grow. Few house plants are as eager to climb as a heartleaf philodendron. If you allow the long stems to grow, put the plant in a hanging basket, or let it trail from a shelf or bookcase. To train it to climb a moss pole, use floral tape to hold the stems up to the pole, until its aerial roots sink in.

It will thrive in a small pot for years with little care. Despite its tropical origins, this beautiful evergreen plant is tolerant of dry air, although it appreciates occasional misting. Keep its leaves clean by wiping them with a damp cloth.

Repot every 2-3 years, in spring or early summer. Use a container with drainage holes to prevent root rot. If you want to use a decorative container without drainage, use it as a cachepot—just slip your plain nursery pot into the cachepot. I like to cover the bottom of a cachepot with pebbles to keep the plant above the drainage water.

Plant Care Tips

- **Origin:** South America
- **Height:** Climbs or trails to 4 ft (1.2 m) or more.
- **Light:** Moderate to bright light, but no direct sun. Will tolerate low light.
- **Water:** Keep soil lightly moist spring through fall. Allow surface to dry out between waterings in winter. Yellow leaves are caused by overwatering.
- **Humidity:** Tolerant of dry air, but likes humidity. Mist foliage occasionally.
- **Temperature:** Average room temperature 60-75°F/16-24°C
- **Soil:** Peat moss-based potting mix.
- **Fertilizer:** Feed monthly spring through fall with a balanced liquid fertilizer diluted by half.
- **Propagation:** Take stem tip cuttings in spring or early summer. It roots easily in water or moist soil.

39

Iron Cross Begonia

Botanical Name: ***Begonia masoniana***

Iron cross begonia leaves are easily recognizable. Each bright-green puckered leaf is marked with a reddish-brown iron-cross pattern in the centre.

You may see sprays of pinkish-white flowers in spring and summer, but these blooms are insignificant compared to the magnificent foliage. Pinching off flower buds will promote bigger, healthier leaves.

If your plant suddenly collapses and shrivels up, don't give up on it. It's not uncommon for this begonia to go dormant in winter. While it's tempting to overwater a withered plant — stop watering during dormancy. What this handsome begonia really craves is high humidity. Cover the plant with plastic or a glass cloche and keep the plant around 60ºF/16ºC for 6-8 weeks. You'll see new leaves appear.

Plant Care Tips

- **Shed some light.** Give your begonia bright, indirect light. You'll get the best leaf colour this way. It thrives under fluorescent lights.
- **Repot in spring.** Move your plant up to a pot only 1 size larger. Using a small pot with a drainage hole will help

to prevent overwatering. Tamp down the soil gently with your fingers so that it doesn't pack too tightly — begonias like a little air around their roots.

- **Don't overwater.** This is one of the few problems with growing begonias. *Begonia masoniana* has rhizomatous roots that store water, so allow the soil to dry out slightly between waterings.

  Also watch for powdery mildew on leaves and stems. Poor air circulation and high humidity are favourable conditions for this dusty, white fungus. Cut off affected leaves and be sure your plant has air circulation around it. However, keep it away from heat/AC vents, which can be drying. Treat foliage with a fungicide when needed.
- **Origin:** Southeast Asia
- **Height:** Up to 1 ft (30 cm)
- **Light:** Bright, indirect light. It also thrives under fluorescent lights.
- **Water:** Water thoroughly, allowing the top 1 in (2.5 cm) of soil to dry out between waterings. Avoid getting water on the leaves because they spot easily and are prone to mildew.
- **Humidity:** Moderate to high humidity. Use a room humidifier or place pot on a tray of wet pebbles to increase humidity. Keep plant away from drafts.
- **Temperature:** Average room temperatures 65-75°F/18-24°C. Begonias are not cold-tolerant and can be damaged by temperatures below 50°F/13°C.
- **Soil:** African violet potting mix.
- **Fertilizer:** Feed monthly year-round with a 10-10-5 liquid fertilizer diluted by half. Fertilize when the soil is already moist to avoid fertilizer burn. Don't feed a dormant plant.
- **Propagation:** Stem cuttings root easily. Take 3 in (8 cm) stem cuttings with leaves in early summer and root them in moist, sterile potting mix. Cover with plastic or a glass cloche to raise humidity around it until new leaves form.

40

'Janet Craig' Dracaena

Botanical Name: ***Dracaena deremensis***

'Janet Craig' is one of the few plants that have taken on the name of a cultivar as a common name. But then, few are as easy to grow and welcome in the home as this attractive Dracaena plant. Its dramatic form makes a striking floor plant.

"Janet" is well worth getting to know. Although tropical by nature, it adapts beautifully to average home conditions. In fact, it does so well on its own, you don't need to fuss over it at all.

Young plants are a tuft of upright leaves. As the plant grows, it forms a cane-like stem with a cluster of leaves at its top.

Its dark-green leaves are naturally shiny. Because of their upright form, they can be dust-catchers. Keep the leaves clean by wiping them off with a damp cloth.

Prune it back if it grows too tall. If you want, you can propagate the stem cuttings for more plants.

Pruning Tips

Prune in spring or early summer to control its growth. You can cut off the cane at any height. It will sprout a new cluster of leaves from where it was cut.

Repot in spring only when the roots have filled the pot. Young plants may need repotted every 2-3 years. Use a pot with a drainage hole to prevent overwatering.

Problems with this *Dracaena* are few. Watch for webbing between leaves. Spider mites may attack during the winter months when the air is dry. Unfortunately, they're difficult to detect until the infestation is severe. Treat your plant right away with insecticidal soap.

Plant Care Tips

- **Origin:** Tropical East Africa
- **Height:** Up to 10 ft (3 m) if not pruned back
- **Light:** Moderate to bright light. Keep plant out of direct sunlight which can scorch its leaves, leaving brown marks. Pale leaves can indicate that light is too low.
- **Water:** This Dracaena plant will tolerate many abuses, but not soggy soil. Water thoroughly, allowing the top inch (2.5 cm) of the soil to dry out between waterings. Use a pot with a drainage hole to prevent wet soil.
- **Humidity:** 40-60 per cent relative humidity
- **Temperature:** Average room temperatures (60-75°F/ 16-24°C)
- **Soil:** Any good potting mix.
- **Fertilizer:** Feed monthly year-round with a balanced liquid fertilizer diluted by half.
- **Propagation:** Take 4 in (10 cm) stem tip cuttings in spring and root them in moist soil.

41

Japanese Aralia

Botanical Name: ***Fatsia japonica***

Japanese aralia is a member of the Araliaceae family commonly grown outdoors in frost-free climates. Indoors, it can be kept small by regular pruning. Cut it back drastically in spring—by half when necessary—and pinch off growing tips to encourage branching.

Long, upright leaf stems hold glossy, lobed leaves with pointed tips. Each leaf has between 7-9 lobes and can reach up to 12 in (30 cm) across. Clusters of creamy-white flowers may appear on mature plants in fall, followed by green fruit that turn black as they ripen. However, it rarely flowers indoors.

This fast-growing, evergreen shrub is easy to care for. It seems to shrug off pests and diseases, and needs little attention to thrive. You can keep it happy by watering regularly and providing good drainage. Overwatering can cause root rot.

You can move it outdoors in summer if you want. Just be sure to put it in a shaded spot outside, because direct sun can burn its leaves.

This plant needs a rest in winter. Move it to a cool spot where the temperature doesn't dip below 45°F/7°C and water less frequently.

Plant Care Tips

- **Origin:** Japan
- **Height:** To 6 ft (1.8 m) indoors
- **Light:** Bright light; no direct summer sun.
- **Water:** Keep soil evenly moist spring through fall, slightly drier in winter.
- **Humidity:** Average indoor humidity.
- **Temperature:** 50-55°F/10-13°C nights; 60-65°F/16-18°C days.
- **Soil:** Any good potting mix.
- **Fertilizer:** Feed every 2 weeks spring and summer with a balanced liquid fertilizer diluted by half.
- **Propagation:** Take stem cuttings in spring.

42

Jerusalem Cherry Pepper

Botanical Name: *Solanum pseudocapsicum*

Branches loaded with brightly coloured peppers make Jerusalem Cherry a favourite ornamental indoor plant in fall and winter.

White, star-shaped flowers cover this shrubby plant in summer.

Beginning in fall, the flowers are followed by small, round fruits that turn from green to yellow to orange to red as they slowly ripen. They are long-lasting and will "decorate" the plant right through the winter.

Although the peppers look a lot like cherry tomatoes, and may seem tempting, the peppers are poisonous and should not be eaten.

Plant Care Tips

- **Let the sun shine in.** Jerusalem Cherry makes an attractive patio plant, where it will get the direct sun it needs to grow, flower and produce peppers. Just be sure to bring your plant back inside before the temperature drops in autumn. This South American native is frost-tender.

- **Give it a rest.** After the fruit is no longer attractive, cut the stems back by half. Reduce watering, but don't allow the soil to dry out completely. Place the plant in a cooler spot (around 60°/16°C). In late spring, move it back to a sunny window—or outdoors after the last threat of frost has passed—and resume normal care.
- **Got a reluctant bloomer?** Plants that don't bloom usually aren't getting enough light. The cool rest followed by a warm, sunny summer should trigger a flush of new flowers followed by peppers. Don't forget to fertilize during the growing season. Plants grown in pots need to be fed regularly. Got blooms, but no peppers? Plants kept for a second year may bloom, but not produce peppers because they aren't pollinated. Don't worry—it's easy to do.
- **How to pollinate your plant:** Plants grown outdoors get pollinated from the wind or insects that carry the pollen from flower to flower. If you've kept your plant indoors, it needs some help from you. Use a small, clean paintbrush to dab the stamens in the centre of the flowers, moving from flower to flower to spread the pollen around.
- **Repot root-bound plants in spring.** Move up to a pot 1 size bigger to give it a little space. Use a pot with a drainage hole to prevent overwatering, which can lead to root rot.
- **Deal with pests.** Something bugging your plant? Jerusalem Cherry is sometimes infested by aphids, whiteflies or spider mites. Regular misting with tepid water will help to prevent an infestation of spider mites, which prefer hot, dry conditions. Use an insecticide, if needed. Organic neem oil insecticide is an effective treatment for many pests.
- **Origin:** Brazil
- **Height:** 1-2 ft (30-60 cm)
- **Light:** Bright light to full sun

- **Water:** Keep the soil evenly moist. Reduce watering in spring, when the plant is resting.
- **Humidity:** Average to moderate room humidity. Mist the plant every day in summer and stand the pot on a tray of wet pebbles. Keep the plant away from heat/air vents. Blasts of dry air will cause the peppers to shrivel and fall off early.
- **Temperature:** Average room temperatures 60-75°F, 16-24°C. If you move your plant outdoors for the summer, don't worry—it can take the heat. If won't, however, tolerate frost. In the fall and winter months, keeping it on the cool side will help the fruit to last longer.
- **Soil:** Any good potting mix.
- **Fertilizer:** Feed monthly spring through fall with a tomato fertilizer.
- **Propagation:** Stem cuttings or seeds. Take stem cuttings in spring and root them in moist potting mix. Gather seeds from ripe fruits and sow in early spring.

43

Kentia Palm

Botanical Name: ***Howea forsteriana***

Over many years, a kentia palm tree can reach several feet in height, making it a striking, tropical floor plant. Give it some elbow room, too. Those elegant, arching fans can grow as much as 1 ft (30 cm) wide and 2 ft (60 cm) long.

All kentia palms grow from a single trunk, but growers typically plant several together for a lush, full appearance.

This is hands-down the most popular indoor palm tree, and it's easy to see why.

The palm family is large, but only a few kinds of palm trees are tolerant of average home conditions. This dramatic palm is one.

How to Care for Kentia Palm Indoors

- **Shed some light.** Kentias tolerate shade better than some, but you'll get a healthier, greener plant by giving your palm bright, indirect light year-round. Take care not to put it in direct sunlight, which may cause brown scorch marks on its leaves.

Cleaning Tips

- Wipe off leaves with a damp cloth every couple weeks or so to keep them dust-free.

- **Give it a shower.** Keep the fronds dust-free by giving your palm a shower. This has the added benefit of flushing the soil of built-up fertilizer. Use a gentle flow of tepid water. Or, stand the plant outdoors for a gentle summer (warm) rain shower. Remember to keep your palm out of direct sun.
- **Repot only when needed.** Planting palm trees is only necessary every 3 years at the most. Kentias are slow-growing and don't like to be disturbed. Their roots are fragile, so handle them with care.

Plant Care Tips

- **Origin:** Lord Howe Island (Northeast of Australia)
- **Height:** Grows slowly, but can reach up to 8 ft (2.4 m) indoors.
- **Light:** Bright, indirect sunlight
- **Water:** Keep soil evenly moist spring through fall; slightly drier in winter.
- **Humidity:** Moderate to high humidity. Use a humidity tray or mist the foliage regularly. You may need to use a room humidifier, especially in the winter.
- **Temperature:** Average room temperatures 60-75°F/ 16-24°C.
- **Soil:** Peat moss-based potting mix with added sand for quick drainage.
- **Fertilizer:** Feed once in spring and once in summer with a slow-release fertilizer. Don't feed in fall and winter when growth has slowed.
- **Propagation:** Seeds.

44

Lady Palm

Botanical Name: ***Rhapis excelsa***

Lady Palm is a dramatic, tall house plant that is easy to grow.

Fronds grow in a fan pattern, each consisting of deeply veined leaflets that grow up to 12 inches (30 cm) long and 1 inch (2.5 cm) wide.

You'll find that the number of leaflets on each stem will vary — typically 5 to 10 — but that just adds to this beautiful palm's appeal. In fact, I've never seen two Lady Palms exactly alike.

A member of the palm family, this elegant-looking plant grows in a clump of woody, upright stems.

As the lower leaves fall off, they leave scars on the stems, creating an attractive bamboo-like appearance.

- **Repot in spring:** Only every 3-4 years, or when this palm outgrows its container. This plant grows best when slightly root-bound, so keep it in a smallish container. Keeping Lady Palm confined to a small container will also dramatically limit its size. In fact, it can be grown in a bonsai pot. When the tree grows to more than 3 ft (90 cm) tall, top dress instead.

- **How to top-dress a plant:** Remove the top 2-3 inches of soil and replace with fresh soil every couple years. Take care not to harm any roots that may be near the surface.
- **Keep it moist:** Palms are *not* desert plants. Aim to keep the soil evenly moist, but not soggy, during the growing season. Mist the foliage daily or use a room humidifier if the air is dry. Brown leaf tips are caused by irregular watering and dry air. Snip off the brown tips with scissors, if you want.

This is a slow-growing palm so buy one the size you want. With good care you'll enjoy it for many years.

Plant Care Tips

- **Origin:** Southeast China.
- **Height:** Up to 10 ft (3 m) outdoors. It stays smaller when grown in a container. In fact, it can be grown as a bonsai plant, reaching only 12 in (30 cm) high.
- **Light:** Bright, indirect light. Too much sun will cause the leaves to turn yellow-green.
- **Water:** Keep soil evenly moist in spring and summer. In winter, allow the top 1 in (2.5 cm) to dry out between waterings. Like other palms, it is sensitive to fluoride and other chemicals in tap water, causing leaf tips to turn brown.
- **Humidity:** High humidity.
- **Temperature:** Average room temperatures 60-75°F/ 16-24°C
- **Soil:** Peat moss based potting mix.
- **Fertilizer:** Feed monthly in summer with a balanced liquid fertilizer diluted by half, or a light sprinkling of time-released house plant fertilizer.
- **Propagation:** Seeds or division.

45

Lucky Bamboo House Plants

Botanical Name: ***Dracaena sanderiana***

Lucky Bamboo first hit the garden centres in the late 1990s. Care for indoor bamboo plant couldn't be easier: it will grow in a vase of water with pebbles to keep it upright.

This striking bamboo plant has a slender, upright stem and graceful, arching green leaves that taper to a point. Its roots are red — so don't worry if you see red roots in the vase. This is normal for a healthy plant.

It's not really a bamboo. This member of the *Dracaena* family has been around a long time, but has become a favourite of feng shui enthusiasts because it is believed to enhance chi energy and bring good luck.

How to Care for Lucky Bamboo

Give your bamboo house plant bright light to help it look its best, but keep this plant out of direct sun to avoid burning its foliage.

It's a good idea to use an opaque vase. Sunlight coming through clear glass will encourage the growth of algae. If the water becomes murky, just clean the vase and pebbles and refill it with clear water.

- **Indoor bamboo problems are few:** Yellow leaves are usually caused by too much sun or too much fertilizer. Cut back on fertilizer and move your bamboo plant to a shadier spot. Brown leaves indicate dry air or chemicals present in the water. Stalks that turn soft and mushy are probably beyond saving. Remove them right away to avoid contaminating the other stalks. If you want to try to save them, you can cut off the mushy parts and place the trimmed stalks in fresh water.
- **Lucky bamboo pruning** will keep your plant in good shape. Don't cut the main stalk—just cut the offshoots within 1-2 in (2.5-5 cm) of the main stalk. This will cause new shoots to grow, creating a fuller, bushier plant. Don't throw those cuttings away, either—root them in fresh water to start new plants.

Wondering how to make those twists and curves?

Although often compared to bonsai, this bamboo house plant is not shaped with wire and frequent trimming. Instead, it is shaped by rotating the plant's stalks. Turning a stalk slowly and regularly in front of a light source naturally causes the stalk to grow toward the light. This is a labour-intensive process and difficult to do in the home.

Plant Care Tips

- **Origin:** Africa
- **Height:** Up to 3 ft (90 cm)
- **Light:** Bright light, but no direct sun which will scorch leaves.
- **Water:** Change the water every week or two. This plant is sensitive to chlorine, fluoride, and other chemicals often found in tap water. Use only distilled or bottled water, or allow tap water to sit overnight so the chemicals will evaporate.
- **Humidity:** Average room humidity.
- **Temperature:** Normal room temperatures. 60-75°F/ 16-24°C

- **Soil:** N/A
- **Fertilizer:** Feed every 2 months with a balanced liquid fertilizer. Just a drop will do.
- **Propagation:** Take stem cuttings in summer and stand in fresh water.

46

Maidenhair Fern

Botanical Name: ***Adiantum raddianum***

Maidenhair Fern is a foliage plant with arching, black, wiry fronds covered with green triangular leaflets, called *pinnae*.

One of the most commonly grown in a container, *Adiantum raddianum* is well-worth growing for its stunning foliage. It will live a long time, too, if you can meet its need for high humidity.

This beautiful fern grows from rhizomes, that spread quickly just under the surface of the soil. It can reach a width of 24 in (60 cm) or more. You'll enjoy many plants over time by propagating this fern. It's easy to divide.

Repot in spring when it has outgrown its pot, using a container that provides good drainage. This is a good time to divide the fern, if needed.

Not many pests bother Maidenhair Fern. However, scale insects and mealybugs are the most common. Check the fronds regularly for infestations. They are much easier to remedy if caught early.

Somewhat difficult to grow, this tropical native demands high humidity which is not practical in most homes. Grows best in terrariums where humidity is kept at a high level. Drafts and dry air will cause leaflets to shrivel.

Pruning Tips

Cut the stems off at the base if the leaflets dry up or fall off. Keep soil moist and raise the humidity around the fern to encourage new growth. Mist twice a day until new shoots appear.

Plant Care Tips

- **Origin:** Brazil and Venezuela
- **Height:** 6-15 inches (15-38 cm).
- **Light:** Moderate to bright light. No direct sun.
- **Water:** Keep soil evenly moist, but not soggy.
- **Humidity:** Requires moist air. Use a humidifier or plant in a terrarium.
- **Temperature:** Average room temperatures 60-75°F/ 16-24°C.
- **Soil:** Combine half potting mix with half peat moss. Don't use potting mix that contains fertilizer (it can dissolve too fast and burn delicate fern roots).
- **Fertilizer:** Feed once a month spring through summer with liquid fertilizer diluted by half.
- **Propagation:** Division. This fern grows from rhizomes that spread horizontally just beneath the surface of the soil. Divide clump in spring, leaving rhizome attached to 1-2 fronds, and pot in its own container.

47

Sensitive Plant

Botanical Name: ***Mimosa pudica***

It won't giggle like Elmo, but Sensitive Plant has a big reaction to being tickled. Its leaves quickly fold up — and the entire stem collapses — when touched, making it a fascinating plant to watch. The leaves also fold up if the plant is shaken or exposed to heat. In fact, high temperatures (75-85°F 24-29°C) may trigger the leaves to close.

It only takes a few minutes, though, for the leaves to slowly unfold and the stems to straighten up.

The feathery, fern-like leaves are made up of 25 pairs of tiny leaflets.

The foliage is attractive on its own, but you'll be captivated by the profusion of pink pompon flowers that bloom from summer into fall.

Mimosa pudica is a perennial shrub, but is often treated like an annual and tossed out, because it tends to deteriorate after flowering. Younger plants are more beautiful, anyway, and sensitive plant seed is quick and easy to grow.

Put your potted plant outside for the summer, if you want, to give it the light it needs. Just don't plant it in the garden. It's considered invasive in warm-climate areas and will spread like a weed.

Plant Care Tips

- **Origin:** Central and South Americas
- **Height:** Up to 2 ft (60 cm)
- **Light:** Bright light with some direct sun.
- **Water:** Keep soil evenly moist, not soggy.
- **Humidity:** Moderate to high humidity. Use a humidity tray.
- **Temperature:** Average room temperatures 65-75°F/ 18-24°C.
- **Soil:** Peat moss based potting mix that drains well.
- **Fertilizer:** Feed every 2 weeks with a high-potassium liquid fertilizer diluted by half while plant is growing.
- **Propagation:** Seeds. Sow sensitive plant seed in early spring. The seed coatings are tough and need scarification to help germinate. Use a sharp knife to (gently) nick the seed coating to expose the white inside of the seed. Barely cover the seeds with potting mix. Keep the medium moist and warm. Seeds should germinate in about a week.

48

Ming Aralia

Botanical Name: ***Polyscias fruticosa***

Ming aralia only *looks* fussy. Its stems carry compound leaves made up of several leaflets, giving the fancy, finely cut foliage an elegant quality you'd expect from a high-maintenance plant.

Fortunately for us, this tropical native is extremely adaptable to most homes.

Put it in full sun — or indirect light. It's quite happy just about anywhere. Keep this aralia plant warm, though. It doesn't like cold temperatures at all. (Who can blame it?)

Plant Care Tips

- **Prune:** Ming aralia has an upright habit and won't grow very tall. Over time, it will drop its lower leaves, revealing a gnarled tree-like trunk. If you want, you can keep it short and shrubby by cutting it back every spring. You'll make it even more beautiful with regular pruning. Prune off the growing tips to encourage branching and denser foliage. Trimming Ming aralia bonsai plant will keep it at 1 ft (30 cm) or less.
- **Repot in spring** only when it has outgrown its pot. Use the smallest pot that will hold its roots — aralias grow

best when their roots are confined. Pot taller plants in a heavy container to prevent toppling. Mings are easily killed by overwatering, so use a pot with a drainage hole.

- **Leaf drop.** If your Ming suddenly starts shedding leaves, don't panic. Some leaf drop is normal. Is it growing new leaves at the stem tips? If so, this is just part of the normal growth. A sudden change in light, such as moving your plant to a shadier location, may cause leaf drop. Give it as much light as you can. Raising the humidity around it can help, too.

Problems with this plant are few. It even seems to shrug off pests. Keep this tropical plant warm and don't overwater — and you'll enjoy it for many years.

If you're looking for a beautiful floor plant, give Ming aralia a try. But be warned, this easy-care house plant just may spoil you for anything else.

- **Origin:** Polynesia.
- **Height:** Up to 3 ft (90 cm); can be grown as a bonsai tree.
- **Light:** Aim for bright light, though it will tolerate varying levels from low light to full sun.
- **Water:** Water thoroughly and allow top 2 in (5 cm) of soil to dry out between waterings. Overwatering is a sure way to kill it. Mings have fine roots and are prone to root rot, so when in doubt, keep it on the dry side. Also cut back on water in the winter when growth has slowed.
- **Humidity:** Moderate to high humidity. If the air is dry, mist the plant every morning or stand the pot on a tray of wet pebbles.
- **Temperature:** Average room temperatures 65-85°F/ 18-29°C. It can take warmer temperatures, but don't expose it to anything below 60°.
- **Soil:** Peat moss-based potting mix with perlite added for good drainage.

- **Fertilizer:** Feed monthly spring through fall with a balanced liquid fertilizer (such as 10-10-10) diluted by half. Young leaves that are yellowish-green are caused by a lack of nutrients.
- **Propagation:** Take 4 in (10 cm) stem tip cuttings in late spring or summer. Cut just below a leaf node (the place where the leaf attaches to the stem) and remove the lower leaves from the cutting. For best results, dip cut end in hormone rooting powder before inserting in moist potting mix. Cover with a plastic bag to hold in the humidity. Keep as warm as possible and out of direct sunlight. It can take a few weeks to root, so be patient.

49

Money Tree Plant

Botanical Name: *Pachira aquatica*

Money tree plant care is easy. Just put it where it'll get some indirect sunlight. Water thoroughly and allow the soil to dry out a bit between waterings. Cut back on water in the winter when growth slows. Use a container with drainage holes and take care not to overwater your plant because it can get root rot.

Its thin trunks are often braided by growers to add to its appeal. Each spoke-like leaf has five bright-green leaflets.

- **Don't overpot:** Use a smallish container because a too-big container will hold too much water. Soggy potting mix is often the biggest problem with this plant, causing stem and root rot and yellowing/dropping leaves. Growing money tree in a small container will also prevent it from getting too big. In fact, this tree can be grown as a bonsai. Regular pruning will also help control its size. Pinch or prune off growing tips.
- **Give it a winter rest:** Keep your money tree warm and in bright light year-round. But cut back on water and stop fertilizing in the winter months because growth slows down with lower light levels.

- **Brown, crispy leaves** is a symptom of dry air or low light levels. Plants often are in shock when moved to a new home because they are adjusting to a new environment. Keep your plant away from heat/AC vents and cold drafts from windows or doorways.
- **Dropped leaves** are also caused by relocation shock. If your new tree drops its leaves, don't give up on it. They'll grow back with good care. Place your money tree in a bright location and leave it there. Increasing humidity around the plant can help. While it's tempting to overwater a shedding plant, don't. It only makes the problem worse.

According to feng shui, money tree will bring good luck and fortune. No, your money tree plant won't actually grow currency, but it is a good investment. Treat it well, and you'll enjoy this delightful tree for many years.

Plant Care Tips

- **Origin:** Central and South America
- **Height:** Up to 10 ft (3 m) tall
- **Light:** Bright light, but no direct sun. Thrives under fluorescent light.
- **Water:** Money tree plant likes water in big gulps. Water thoroughly, until water comes out the drainage holes in the bottom of the pot, then allow the top 1-2 inches (2.5-5 cm) to dry out between waterings. Avoid getting water on the trunk, which causes stem rot. Water less in winter.
- **Humidity:** Moderate to high. Try to keep the relative humidity at 50 per cent or higher. Set the pot on a tray of wet pebbles to raise the humidity around it.
- **Temperature:** Average room temperatures 60-75°F/ 16-24°C.
- **Soil:** Use a peat moss-based potting mix with perlite or sand added for good drainage.

- **Fertilizer:** Feed every 2 weeks in spring and summer with a balanced liquid fertilizer diluted by half.
- **Propagation:** Seeds or stem tips. Take stem tip cuttings in spring, with at least 2 leaf nodes attached. Dip the cut end in rooting hormone powder then place it in moist potting mix. Be patient—it can take several weeks to root.

50

Moses in the Cradle

Botanical Name: ***Tradescantia spathacea***

Moses in the Cradle is a popular house plant, related to the Wandering Jew plant. You'll find that it's just as easy to grow.

Dark-green, lance-shaped leaves with purplish-red undersides make this a beautiful house plant year-round. Pot it in a small decorative container for a stunning table accent. A newer variety, *Rhoea discolour* 'Variegata' is even more spectacular, with striped foliage in burgundy, pink, green and cream.

It blooms any time of year. Small, white, 3-petaled flowers grow in the leaf axils, nestled in the boat-shaped leaves, giving this plant its common names.

Plant Care Tips

- **Let the sun shine in.** Grow your plant in bright light year-round for good foliage colour and flowers. It will tolerate lower light, but the leaves will be more green than purple.
- **Raise the humidity in winter** by misting the foliage with tepid water daily, or using a humidifier. Place the pot on a tray of wet pebbles to keep the air moist around it.

- **Repot in spring** when the plant becomes crowded, probably every couple years. Move up to a pot only 1 size larger to give it a little room to grow. Use a pot with drainage holes to prevent soggy soil, which leads to root rot.
- **Origin:** Mexico
- **Height:** 1-2 ft (30-60 cm)
- **Light:** Bright light, but no direct sun.
- **Water:** Keep soil evenly moist year-round.
- **Humidity:** Average room humidity. Brown leaf tips indicate that the air is too dry. Mist the foliage with room-temperature water or stand the pot on a humidity tray.
- **Temperature:** Average to warm room temperatures (65-80°F/18-27°C) suit this plant year-round.
- **Soil:** Good-quality all-purpose potting mix.
- **Fertilizer:** Feed monthly in spring and summer with a balanced (10-10-10) liquid fertilizer diluted by half.
- **Propagation:** Division. Remove offshoots with some roots attached and pot separately.

51

Nerve Plant

Botanical Name: ***Fittonia verschaffeltii***

Nerve Plant has beautiful, deep-green leaves with vein patterns of white, pink, or red.

In its native South America, this tropical plant grows as a ground cover and can spread out about 12 inches (30 cm). Its low-spreading habit makes it ideal for dish gardens and terrariums, where it thrives with the help of high humidity.

This plant grows best with even temperatures around 70°F/21°C. It doesn't like dry air, drafts, or direct sun, any of which may cause its leaves to shrivel or fall off.

Group your Plants

Nerve Plant grows beautifully in a dish garden or a terrarium. Combine it with 2 or 3 of these humidity-loving plants:

- Parlor Palm
- Heartleaf Philodendron
- Arrowhead Plant
- English Ivy
- **Pinch your plant:** Pinch off stems tips regularly to keep plant bushy and full. Also pinch off any small flower

spikes that may appear, because they are insignificant and will weaken the show of leaves.

- **Mist it:** This tropical beauty loves to be misted. Give it a fine spray of tepid water every morning to provide the moist air it craves. Or, place the pot on a tray of wet pebbles to raise the humidity around it.
- **Repot in spring:** Every couple years to refresh the soil. Nerve Plant has shallow roots, so you can keep it in a small pot.

Plant Care Tips

- **Origin:** Peru
- **Height:** Up to 6 in (15 cm)
- **Light:** Low to medium light. Avoid direct sunlight. Grows well under fluorescent light.
- **Water:** Keep soil constantly moist, but not soggy. Plant will collapse if it dries out.
- **Humidity:** High humidity (above 70% relative humidity). Grows best in terrariums.
- **Temperature:** Average room temperatures 65-75°F, 18-24°C
- **Soil:** Peat-based potting mix that holds moisture well.
- **Fertilizer:** Feed every 2-3 months spring through fall with a balanced liquid fertilizer.
- **Propagation:** Take 2 in (5 cm) stem tip cuttings in spring and insert them in moist potting mix. They propagate easily in a warm, humid environment, rooting in about 2-3 weeks.

52

Norfolk Island Pine

Botanical Name: ***Araucaria heterophylla***

Norfolk Island pine is an evergreen conifer that makes a handsome house plant. Its long, horizontal branches are densely covered with short, soft needles that become darker as the plant ages.

This plant not a true pine, it just looks like one. It also gets its name from Norfolk Island — a small island in the Pacific between Australia, New Zealand and New Caledonia.

In its native habitat, Norfolk Island pine can grow up to 200 ft (60 m) tall. As a house plant, you can expect it to reach about 3-6 ft (90 cm - 1.8 m). Slow-growing, it will take several years to reach this height.

To understand how to care for these plants, remember their native environment, where they enjoy moderate temperatures, moist air and bright light. Dry air, dry soil and low light can cause the needles to drop—and they won't grow back. They need a little extra attention, but they're worth it. Norfolk pine trees will live a long time with good care.

Plant Pine Care

- **Raise the humidity:** Dry air will cause the needles to become dry and fall off. Keep your plant away from heat/

AC vents. This Pacific Island native loves to be misted with room-temperature water. Or, use a room humidifier to add moisture.

- **Keep soil moist:** Growing Norfolk Island pine trees are thirsty, so check the soil often during the growing season. Yellow needles are typically caused by soil that's either too dry or soggy. Aim to keep it lightly moist at all times.
- **Repot in spring:** This plant is slow-growing, especially indoors. Move it into a pot 1 size larger every 3 years or when roots are visible on top of the soil. When the tree grows to more than 3 ft (90 cm) tall, top dress instead.
- **Don't prune Norfolk pine:** Never cut off the top or trim the sides of this plant. It doesn't need to be shaped at all. You can remove any lower branches that die, using sharp pruners to prevent tearing the stems.

Not many house plant pests bother Norfolk pines. Mealybugs are the most common. Watch for white, cotton-like areas on leaves and stems and treat any infestation immediately.

- **Origin:** Norfolk Island
- **Height:** 6 ft (1.8 m)
- **Light:** Bright light with some full sun.
- **Water:** Keep the soil evenly moist in the spring and summer, lightly moist in winter.
- **Humidity:** Moderate room humidity.
- **Temperature:** Average room temperatures 60-75°F, 16-24°C.
- **Soil:** Any good potting mix.
- **Fertilizer:** Feed every 2 weeks spring through fall with a balanced liquid fertilizer diluted by half.
- **Propagation:** Can be grown from seed, although it will take several years to reach the size of a purchased plant.

53

Ornamental Pepper Plant

Botanical Name: ***Capsicum annuum***

Grown for its brightly coloured fruit, ornamental pepper plant is not particularly attractive until it becomes loaded with ripening peppers in fall and winter. Another common name for this plant is Christmas Pepper.

C. annuum puts on a spectacular display when covered with a bounty of colourful peppers. However, it's a one-time production. You can expect ornamental peppers to produce fruit for up to 6 weeks. It will not bear fruit again and is usually treated as a temporary house plant and discarded when it is no longer attractive.

White, star-shaped flowers grow in the leaf axils in summer and early fall, followed by the real star of the show — colourful peppers.

They may be cone-shaped or round, depending on the variety. But, the peppers all change colours as they mature — from green to yellow to orange to red. Some varieties have purple fruit that is almost black.

- **'Black Pearl'**, shown at left, is a popular cultivar with unusual dark foliage, making this a striking ornamental.
- **Pinch your plant:** Pinch new growth to encourage the stems to branch out and become bushy.

- **Some like it hot:** Keep this tropical native warm. Ornamental chili pepper is tender and should not be exposed to temperatures below 55ºF/13ºC.
- **Caution:** The peppers are edible, but most are fiery hot. The juice from them can cause painful burning of the eyes and mouth. Keep plants away from small children and wash your hands thoroughly after handling the peppers.

Plant Care Tips

- **Origin:** South America.
- **Height:** To 1 ft (30 cm)
- **Light:** Bright light, including at least 4 hours a day of direct sun.
- **Water:** Keep soil evenly moist. Leaves will drop if soil is too wet or too dry. Water thoroughly and discard drainage.
- **Humidity:** Average to moderate humidity. Mist foliage occasionally if needed.
- **Temperature:** Cool at night, 55-60ºF/13-16ºC; warm during the day 70-75ºF/21-24ºC
- **Soil:** Any good potting mix.
- **Fertilizer:** Feed monthly with a balanced liquid fertilizer diluted by half.
- **Propagation:** Seed. Sow seeds in spring.

54

Papyrus Plant

Botanical Name: ***Cyperus papyrus***

Once used by the ancient Egyptians to make paper, papyrus plant is now cultivated as an ornamental in tropical wetlands and as a house plant.

Growing in clumps, the thin papyrus stems are topped with dark-green, grass-like rays that resemble umbrella spokes. Some varieties have fountain-like feathery clusters.

This evergreen plant grows from thick rhizomes. Fast-growing, it's considered a weed in some countries. However, it won't spread too far in a pot.

Papyrus flowers in late summer, when given enough sunlight. The greenish-brown flower clusters appear at the crown of the rayed stems.

Plant Care Tips

Native to wetlands, this exotic-looking plant prefers wet soil so it's almost impossible to overwater. You can leave the pot in a saucer filled with water, if you want. Just don't let this plant dry out. Brown tips are a sign that the soil is dry.

Repot in spring when the roots have filled the pot. Move up only 1 size larger.

- **Photo credit:** Kurt Stueber
- **Origin:** Africa
- **Height:** Up to 10 ft (3 m); dwarf papyrus grows to 2 ft (60 cm)
- **Light:** Full sunlight to low light
- **Water:** Keep the soil evenly moist at all times. Never allow the soil to dry out.
- **Humidity:** Average room humidity
- **Temperature:** Normal room temperatures 60-75°F/ 16-24°C
- **Soil:** Any good potting mix.
- **Fertilizer:** Feed monthly spring through fall with a balanced liquid fertilizer diluted by half. Only fertilize when watering to avoid fertilizer burn.
- **Propagation:** Divide plant in spring. Or, take 4 in (10 cm) stem tip cuttings in spring and root them in water.

55

Parlor Palm

Botanical Name: ***Chamaedorea elegans***

Parlor palm is a popular house plant and easy to care for. Although the palm family is large, only a few make good house plants. *Chamaedorea elegans* is one of those few, adapting beautifully to average indoor conditions.

It has elegant, green leaflets on arching fronds, giving this palm a feathery canopy shape.

Given enough light, a mature plant may produce sprays of small yellow flowers on tall stalks above the foliage. The flowers are followed by seeds that are rarely fertile and not worth saving, so just cut the flowers off when they begin to turn brown.

Although this palm will tolerate dry indoor air, it will be healthier with higher humidity. I mist mine a few times a week with room-temperature water. Misting also keeps its leaves clean and helps to prevent spider mites that love to attack this plant.

- **Do not prune:** Parlor palm grows from a terminal bud. Pruning this single point of growth will cause it to stop growing. However, it's fine to trim off old fronds that have turned brown.

Repot in spring, only when the roots have filled the pot. Always use a pot with drainage holes to prevent soggy soil, which can cause root rot.

This is one of the few palms that grows well in low light. Its tolerance for lack of light and low humidity make it an ideal office plant.

Plant Care Tips

- **Origin:** Mexico
- **Height:** Slow-growing. Fully mature plants may reach 3-4 ft (90 cm - 1.2 m).
- **Light:** Low light to moderately bright light. If leaves are yellowish-green, it may be getting too much sun.
- **Water:** Keep soil lightly moist. Provide good drainage.
- **Humidity:** Mist the foliage regularly to increase humidity.
- **Temperature:** Normal to warm room temperatures 65-80°F/18-27°C.
- **Soil:** Two parts peat moss-based potting mix and one part sharp sand.
- **Fertilizer:** Needs more fertilizer than most palms. Feed monthly in spring and summer with slow-release fertilizer.
- **Propagation:** Seeds.

56

Peacock Plant

Botanical Name: ***Calathea makoyana***

Peacock Plant is a member of the Marantaceae family of prayer plants.

Tall, slender stems hold up the oval leaves that can grow to 12 in (30 cm) long.

The bold, decorative markings of its thin, delicate leaves resemble a peacock's tail, lending this beautiful Calathea plant its common name. They are pale green with feathered dark-green lines from the midrib to the outside edges of the leaf. Asymetrical stripes add an exquisite effect.

New leaves are rolled up when they emerge and are pinkish-red on the undersides.

Plant Care Tips

- **Shun the sun:** Keep this showy calathea plant out of direct sun to avoid dulling the colours of the leaves.
- **Raise the humidity:** Calatheas are fussy about humidity and love to be misted. If the leaves turn yellow or brown, it is likely because the air is too dry. Use every practical way to keep the relative humidity above 60 per cent, especially in winter. I recommend using a humidity tray or room humidifier.

- **Repot in spring:** Move up to a pot 1 size larger when the plant outgrows its pot. This is a good time to divide large, crowded plants. Use a container with drainage holes to avoid overwatering which can lead to root rot.
- **Origin:** Brazil.
- **Height:** Up to 2 ft (60 cm).
- **Light:** Low to moderate light. Keep out of direct sun.
- **Water:** Keep mix evenly moist at all times. Use distilled or rain water because calathea is sensitive to fluoride and other chemicals in many public water supplies.
- **Humidity:** Requires moist air. Set pot on a tray of wet pebbles and mist leaves frequently with room-temperature water.
- **Temperature:** Average to warm room temperatures 70-85°F/21-29°C.
- **Soil:** Peat moss based potting mix.
- **Fertilizer:** Feed monthly with a balanced house plant fertilizer diluted by half spring through fall. Do not feed in winter. New leaves that are lighter in colour aren't getting enough nitrogen or iron. If your fertilizer doesn't contain these nutrients, use a foliar spray that lists these nutrients on the bottle. You should see an improvement within a few weeks.
- **Propagation:** Division. Calathea plant is not easy to divide, so divide the plant in spring only when it gets quite large.

57

Peperomia Caperata

Botanical Name: ***Peperomia caperata***

A member of the Piperaceae family, this compact plant has short stems covered by heart-shaped, deeply ridged leaves. The leaves are green, sometimes with a blush of red, and dark green veins. In summer or fall, it may produce slender flower spikes that look like rat's tails.

Plant Care Tips

Peperomia is easy to grow and usually trouble-free.

- **Don't overwater.** The only thing that really bothers this plant is soggy soil. Allow the soil to dry out slightly between waterings. Water sparingly in winter. Wilting leaves is likely because drainage is poor and its roots are not getting enough oxygen.
- **Repot in spring,** only when the plant has outgrown its pot. Move it into a container that's only slightly larger, because a container that's too big will hold too much water and may cause root rot. Also, be sure to use a container with a drainage hole.
- **Leaf drop** may be caused by a build-up of salts in the soil from soft water or too much fertilizer. You can see

accumulated salts as a white crusty deposits on the surface of the soil. Fortunately, it's easy to flush out excess salts.

- **How to flush out salts:** Pour plenty of room-temperature water over the soil, drenching the soil and allowing the excess water to drain out of the drainage holes for several minutes. Then pour more water. Empty the drainage tray.

Its textured leaves and low-growing mound of foliage make it an ideal addition to a dish garden or a terrarium.

- **Origin:** Brazil
- **Height:** 8 in (20 cm)
- **Light:** Low to bright light. No direct sun. Peperomia thrives under fluorescent grow lights.
- **Water:** Keep soil barely moist. Allow the top inch of soil to dry between waterings. Water less in winter, allowing the top half of the soil to dry out between waterings.
- **Humidity:** Moderate humidity.
- **Temperature:** Average room temperatures 60-75°F/ 16-24°C.
- **Soil:** Light potting mix that contains perlite or sand to help drainage.
- **Fertilizer:** Feed monthly spring through fall with a balanced liquid fertilizer diluted by half.
- **Propagation:** Take leaf cuttings in spring.

58

Persian Shield Plant

Botanical Name: ***Strobilanthes dyerianus***

Persian Shield is a stunning house plant that's a cinch to grow with minimal attention.

Its lance-shaped leaves are deep purple and green with a shimmer of silver. The colours lighten as the plant ages. You may see light-blue flowers appear in summer, but they pale in comparison to the magnificent foliage. Pinch off the flower spikes as soon as you see them to keep the foliage looking its best.

This beautiful soft-stemmed shrub is fast-growing. Cut Persian Shield back in spring when it becomes leggy. Pinching off its stem tips in spring and summer will encourage branching and create a fuller, bushier plant.

- **Pruning tip:** Cut a stem at an angle, just above a node (the place where a leaf or branch is attached to the stem).

  Repot in spring when the roots have filled the pot—probably every couple years.

Plant Care Tips

- **Origin:** Burma (officially, the Union of Myanmar)
- **Height:** Up to 2-3 ft (60-90 cm)

- **Light:** Bright indirect light
- **Water:** Water thoroughly and allow the soil to dry out a bit between waterings. Keep soil drier in winter months, but do not allow it to dry out completely.
- **Humidity:** Average room humidity
- **Temperature:** Normal room temperatures 60-75°F/ 16-24°C.
- **Soil:** Any good potting mix.
- **Fertilizer:** Feed every 2 weeks spring through fall with a balanced liquid fertilizer diluted by half. Only fertilize when watering to avoid fertilizer burn.
- **Propagation:** Take 4 in (10 cm) stem tip cuttings in spring and root them in moist soil. Propagating the cuttings requires a heat mat for best results. Cuttings should root in about 2-3 weeks.

59

Piggyback Plant

Botanical Name: ***Tolmiea menziesii***

In its native habitat, piggyback plant grows as a groundcover in the shady woodland forests along the northern Pacific coastline. Give it a cool spot with high humidity and you'll find it's easy to grow.

The lush, green, hairy leaves on this evergreen are mapleleaf-shaped with scalloped edges. Decorative leaf patterns form an eye-catching mound of foliage. But, the captivating feature is the way it makes new plants. Mature leaves grow new plantlets from the top of its *petioles* (the place where the leaf attaches to the stem). This unusual growth habit lends the common names, piggyback plant, youth-on-age and thousand mothers.

Spikes of tubular flowers sometimes appear in summer, but rarely on plants grown indoors.

Plant Care Tips

- Repot in spring every couple years or when the roots fill the pot. Its creeping roots spread so use a wide pot. Just be sure to use one with drainage holes to prevent overwatering.

- Brown, crispy leaves? Dry-looking foliage can be caused by a few things:
- Direct sun can cause brown scorch marks on the leaves. Keep plant out of strong summer sun.
- Low humidity is likely the culprit. Crispy, shriveled leaves are a sign that the air is too dry. Mist with water, use a pebble tray or a room humidifier to raise the humidity around the plant. High temperatures can send the humidity plummeting, so daily misting may be needed in the summer.
- Dry soil could also cause dry leaves. Aim to keep the soil evenly moist.
- **Pinch your plant** back to keep it from getting leggy. Giving it bright light will help it to grow lush and full.
- **Caution:** The hairs on the leaves and stems can cause minor skin irritation. It's a good idea to wear gloves when repotting or propagating.
- **Origin:** West Coast of North America (From Alaska to Northern California)
- **Height:** Up to 1 ft (30 cm)
- **Light:** Moderate to bright light, but no direct sun.
- **Water:** Water regularly throughout the growing season, keeping the soil evenly moist, but not soggy. Water less in winter, when growth is slower.
- **Humidity:** High humidity. Mist foliage with room-temperature water or use a pebble tray to raise humidity. Brown leaf tips are a sign that the air is too dry.
- **Temperature:** Cool to average room temperatures 50-75°F/10-24°C.
- **Soil:** Any good potting mix.
- **Fertilizer:** Feed monthly in spring and summer with a balanced liquid fertilizer diluted by half.
- **Propagation:** Take leaf cuttings with plantlets and set them in a pot, allowing the base of the plantlets to touch the soil. Roots will form quickly from this junction. After the parent leaf has dried up, cut it away from the newly rooted plantlet.

60

Pitcher Plant Carnivorous

Botanical Name: *Nepenthes* Species and Hybrids

Pitcher Plant care is easy — or difficult — depending on the growing conditions you have available.

Unlike many carnivorous plants that come from bogs and swamps and prefer wet, cool conditions, *Nepenthes* prefers tropical warmth and humidity. So unless you happen to live in the tropics, this epiphytic carnivore will need special accommodations.

A heated sunroom or greenhouse, where the air is consistently warm and humid is the best place for your pitcher plant. Just keep it shaded from direct sunlight at all times. Put it in a hanging basket to show off those unusual and fascinating pitchers.

The glossy green leaves grow to 1 ft (30 cm) long and feature a tendril at the tip. Large, pendulous pitchers commonly grow at the tips of those tendrils and are topped with a lid to keep out the rain. Depending on the species or hybrid, the pitchers may be yellow-green or mid-green and splashed or spotted with purple or red.

About those Bug-eating Pitchers

Because this epiphytic carnivorous plant is unable to get the nutrients it needs from soil, it has developed a way to attract, capture and ingest insects. Bugs are lured inside its pitchers with an intoxicating nectar. Once inside, the insects fall into the pepsin liquid where they drown and are digested.

Repot in spring only when needed. Handle the roots carefully because they're delicate and break easily.

Prune it back in spring to keep the plant a reasonable size. Older plants can be cut back harshly. Pruning encourages new growth so you'll get a fuller plant.

Plant Care Tips

- **Origin:** Borneo and Malaysia
- **Height:** Climbs or trails to 10 ft (3 m)
- **Light:** Moderate to bright light, but no direct sun.
- **Water:** Keep soil evenly moist year-round. Because this plant is sensitive to chemicals in tap water, use only distilled or lime-free rain water.
- **Humidity:** Moderate to high (50-80% relative humidity) is a must for pitcher plant care. Mist the plant every day or use a room humidifier. Pitcher plants grow best in a heated greenhouse.
- **Temperature:** Average to warm 75-85°F/24-29°C. It will tolerate a minimum of 65°F/18°C.
- **Soil:** Use a nutrient-poor medium because rich potting mix will harm its roots. You can plant it in live sphagnum moss, or if that is not available, mix 1 part peat moss with 1 part perlite or sharp sand.
- **Fertilizer:** Don't fertilize the plant. In spring and fall, drop a few insects into the pitchers occasionally if there are none flying around. Don't use bugs that have been treated with insecticide.
- **Propagation:** Take leaf cuttings in spring and root them in sphagnum moss. Use a heat mat. Mist every day with tepid water to keep the medium moist. Be patient — rooting can take up to 8 weeks.

61

Polka Dot Plant

Botanical Name: ***Hypoestes phyllostachya***

Dark green leaves splattered with pink make Polka Dot Plant an unusual and attractive house plant. Newer hybrids are available with red or white spotted leaves.

This bushy plant grows quickly with good light. Pinch back growing tips often to encourage branching and to keep the plant compact.

Insignificant purple flower spikes may appear. Pinch them off because they detract from the foliage and can cause the plant to deteriorate after blooming.

Plant Care Tips

- **Shed some light:** Leaves may revert to solid-green in low light. Put your plant where it'll get plenty of light, but out of direct sun. Filtered light from a south- or west-facing window will give it the light it needs. If you move your plant outdoors for the summer, keep it fully shaded from hot sun, which can cause leaves to curl up and develop brown scorch marks.
- **Keep up the humidity:** If relative humidity drops below 50 per cent, use a humidity tray or room humidifier to

increase the moisture in the air. Grouping plants also helps to maintain the humidity around them. A terrarium is an ideal home for this humidity-loving plant, where it will add eye-catching colour among green foliage plants.

- **Water regularly:** Keep the soil lightly moist, but take care not to overwater. Too-dry soil will cause leaves to wilt and drop off. Quickly revive a wilted plant with a thorough watering. Soggy soil will cause the leaves to turn yellow.
- **Pinch your plant:** Pinch off tall stems to prevent the plant from getting too leggy. Also, pinch off growing tips to encourage stems to branch out for a fuller, bushier plant.
- **Origin:** Madagascar
- **Height:** Keep to about 10 in (25 cm) by pinching off.
- **Light:** Bright light is needed for good leaf colour, but protect plants from direct sun to prevent scorching leaves.
- **Water:** Keep soil evenly moist spring through fall and slightly drier in winter.
- **Humidity:** Likes moist air. A humidifier works well.
- **Temperature:** Average to warm 65-80ºF/18-27ºC.
- **Soil:** Peat moss based potting mix.
- **Fertilizer:** Feed every 2 weeks spring through fall with a balanced liquid fertilizer diluted by half.
- **Propagation:** Grows easily from seeds. Take stem cuttings in spring and early summer.

62

Pothos Golden or Devil's Ivy

Botanical Name: ***Epipremnum aureum***

Extremely easy to grow. Golden pothos is a popular house plant well known for its long, trailing stems that can grow to 8 ft (2.4 m) or more.

Cut them back a couple times a year to keep the plant bushy and full. Cutting right above a leaf node (the place where the leaf is attached to the stem) will encourage the stem to branch out, giving you a fuller plant.

Glossy, heart-shaped leaves emerge green and become variegated with yellow or white. Although this plant tolerates low light well, its leaves may lose their variegation. It will look its best in moderate or bright light. It makes an excellent office plant because it grows well under fluorescent lights.

Air-Cleaning Plant

Pothos is one of the best plants for removing formaldehyde from carpet and other materials in our homes. Beautiful, low-maintenance, and cleans the air. What's not to love?

Its trailing stems make it an attractive plant for a hanging basket. Or you can train it to climb. Pothos has aerial roots that can be trained to climb a moss stick or trellis that is inserted into the soil.

Repot in spring as needed. You can control its growth by cutting the vines back and trimming up to a third of its roots. Pot it in the same size container to keep it small.

Plant Care Tips

- **Origin:** Solomon Islands
- **Height:** To 8 ft (2.4 m)
- **Light:** Low light to bright light. No direct sun.
- **Water:** Allow soil to dry slightly between waterings. It will not tolerate soggy soil.
- **Humidity:** Average room humidity.
- **Temperature:** Average to warm 60-80°F/16-27°C.
- **Soil:** Any good potting mix that drains well.
- **Fertilizer:** Feed every 2 weeks spring through fall with a balanced liquid fertilizer diluted by half. In winter, feed monthly.
- **Propagation:** Stem tip cuttings root easily in water or moist perlite or vermiculite. It takes about 4 weeks.

63

Prayer Plant

Botanical Name: ***Maranta leuconeura***

Prayer Plant earned its name because of the way its leaves fold together at night, like hands closed in prayer. Its leaves unfold in the morning light, sometimes making a rustling sound.

Showy, oval-shaped leaves have a spectacular light-and-dark-green feathered pattern with red veins, and are often red underneath. Its leaves grow to about 5 in (12 cm) long.

Prayer plants rarely bloom indoors, but sometimes grow tiny, white tubular flowers on long stems. The flowers are insignificant, anyway. It's the magnificent leaves that are really the attraction.

You can expect your plant to take a "rest" in winter and growth will slow down. Water lightly during this time and stop fertilizing, but maintain humidity. You can expect a flush of colourful, new leaves to appear in spring and summer.

Pruning Tip

Your plant will benefit from occasional pruning, which helps to give it a nice shape and promote new growth. Fall is the best time to cut it back. Use sharp pruners to cut away some of the older leaves.

Give it good care and it will live for many years. This tropical plant prefers a warm, humid environment and well-aerated soil. To prevent the soil from becoming too compact, repot it every spring. Do not pack the soil tightly around the roots — keep it loose. You can choose a shallow pot for your prayer plant. Its shallow root system doesn't need much room.

Gently wipe leaves with a soft, dry cloth to clean them. Keeping the foliage clean will also deter spider mites or other pests.

Plant Care Tips

- **Origin:** Brazil
- **Height:** Up to 12 inches (30 cm)
- **Light:** Prayer plants will tolerate low light levels, but grow best with bright light. No direct sun.
- **Water:** Keep soil evenly moist spring through summer, slightly drier in winter.
- **Humidity:** Requires moist air. Brown leaf tips are a sign that the air is too dry. Try to maintain at least 50 per cent relative humidity year-round. It's a good idea to use a humidity tray or a room humidifier.
- **Temperature:** Average to warm (65-80°F/18-27°C) year-round.
- **Soil:** Peat-rich potting mix.
- **Fertilizer:** Feed with a liquid fertilizer diluted by half every 2 weeks spring through fall.
- **Propagation:** In spring, take 4-inch (10 cm) stem cuttings with 3-4 leaves attached. Root them in moist potting mix. When your plant gets too big, you can easily divide it in half by pulling apart its shallow roots.

64

Purple Passion Plant or Velvet Plant

Botanical Name: ***Gynura aurantiaca***

Purple Passion Plant is known for its finely serrated green leaves, densely covered with purple hairs.

The leaf undersides and stems are also hairy, giving the whole plant an iridescent, velvety sheen.

Pinch off the yellow-orange flowers that appear in spring. They're not only ugly, they have a bad odor. Plants often flower after they're a year old. You may notice that your plant will begin to decline after flowering. That's why it's a good idea to propagate cuttings to replace your plant. It's fast-growing, so you'll have a big, lush-looking new house plant in no time.

- **Shed some light:** Providing bright light will enhance the colour of this stunning foliage plant. If the leaves are more green than purple, move the plant to a sunnier spot. Keep it out of harsh, direct sunlight, though, because its leaves will scorch.
- **Pinch it back:** Pinching off the stem tips is the way to make it branch out for a fuller, bushier plant. Don't toss out those stem tip cuttings, either. They'll root easily, giving you more beautiful plants.

- **Water regularly:** Purple Passion Plant is a "fainter" if the soil is allowed to dry out. However, you can revive it quickly with a thorough watering. Aim to keep the soil evenly moist during the growing season, slightly drier in winter.

Plant Care Tips

- **Origin:** Indonesia
- **Height:** Upright forms grow to 2 ft (60 cm) tall. Trailing forms can grow to 4 ft (1.2 m) long.
- **Light:** Bright indirect light. Some direct morning sun is fine, but avoid strong summer sun which can scorch its leaves.
- **Water:** Keep the soil evenly moist spring through fall. Water less in winter, keeping the plant barely moist. When watering, take care not to get water drops on the leaves which can damage them.
- **Humidity:** Moderate to high. If the relative humidity drops below 50 per cent, use a pebble tray or room humidifier. Don't mist this plant because the hairs trap moisture that may cause the leaves to rot.
- **Temperature:** Average room temperatures 60-75°F/ 16-24°C.
- **Soil:** Peat moss-based potting mix.
- **Fertilizer:** Feed every 2 weeks spring through fall with a balanced liquid fertilizer diluted by half. Feed monthly in winter.
- **Propagation:** Take 3-4 in (7.5-10 cm) stem tip cuttings in spring or early summer. Cut just below a *node* — the place where a leaf is attached to a stem. Dip cut ends in hormone rooting powder and place in moist peat moss or perlite. Enclose in a clear, plastic bag or cloche for the first couple weeks to hold in moisture.

65

Pygmy Date Palm Tree

Botanical Name: ***Phoenix roebelenii***

Pygmy Date Palm is a dwarf plant reaching only 4 ft tall after several years. Give it some space, though. This slow-growing palm will spread to about 4 ft wide.

Its long, arching fronds feature slender, delicate-looking leaflets. Unlike other date palms, this one has soft leaflets giving it a feathery, elegant look.

There are sharp spines at the bases of the leaflets, so it's a good idea to wear garden gloves when trimming off old fronds.

This plant doesn't require a lot of attention, but be careful not to overwater it. Poor drainage and soggy soil can cause root rot.

Repot a young plant in spring every couple years, to give it the space it needs to grow. When it gets older, just top dress by replacing the top couple inches of soil. This plant has delicate roots and doesn't like to be disturbed. Use a heavy container to prevent it from toppling because this spreading palm gets top-heavy.

Plant Care Tips

- **Origin:** Southeast Asia

- **Height:** Up to 4 ft (1.2 m) indoors
- **Light:** Bright light.
- **Water:** Keep soil moist spring through summer and barely moist in fall and winter.
- **Humidity:** Moderate to high. When the relative humidity drops below 50 per cent, stand the pot on a humidity tray and mist the foliage with room-temperature water.
- **Temperature:** Average to warm 65-85°F/18-29°C.
- **Soil:** Use a potting mix that drains well. I recommend adding perlite or sand to a standard potting mix.
- **Fertilizer:** Feed once in spring and again in summer with a time-release fertilizer. Rose fertilizer works well because it provides the micronutrients this palm needs. A shortage of magnesium will cause yellow spots on the leaflets.
- **Propagation:** Cut off the suckers that grow at the base of the plant. Be sure to include the roots with it, and pot them in separate containers. Plants can be grown from seeds, but you'll wait years for the plant to grow into a tree.

66

Rabbit Foot Fern Care Tips

Botanical Name: ***Davallia fejeensis***

Although most types of ferns require high humidity, Rabbit Foot Fern is much easier to please as indoor ferns. House plants will thrive with indirect light and average room temperatures.

Elegant, lacy fronds create a lush mound of evergreen foliage. The main attraction of this plant, however, are the furry rhizomes that hang over the side of the container. These light-brown, creeping rhizomes are covered with hairs that look like a rabbit's foot. It's a good idea to put the plant in a hanging basket because they can grow up to 2 ft (60 cm) long. And because you want to show them off, don't you?

Those furry rhizomes are more than eye-catching — they take up moisture. Mist them every day — or as needed — with tepid water to prevent them from drying out.

Winter Care

Cut back on watering during the winter months, when growth slows. Put rabbit foot fern in a cooler spot for the winter, but don't expose it to temperatures below 55°F/13°C. Keep it away from heat vents and drafts.

This Pacific island native tends to lose some of its leaflets in winter. This is normal, and don't worry...this vigorous plant will replace them. Raising the humidity can help.

Repot in spring only when it gets crowded in its pot. Rabbit's foot fern has a shallow root system, so move it to a shallow pot only 1-2 in (2.5-5 cm) wider. Keep the furry rhizomes on the soil surface because if you bury them, they'll easily rot. This is a good time to divide the plant, if you want.

Plant Care Tips

- **Origin:** Fiji
- **Height:** 18 in (46 cm)
- **Light:** Moderate to bright light. Keep it out of direct sun, which will scorch its leaflets. Fluorescent light works well, too.
- **Water:** Spring through fall, keep the soil moist, but not soggy. In winter, allow top 1 in (2.5 cm) of soil to dry out between waterings.
- **Humidity:** Moderate humidity. Use a room humidifier or place pot on a tray of wet pebbles to raise the humidity around it. This fern also loves to be misted.
- **Temperature:** Average room temperatures 60-75°F, 16-24°C spring through fall. In winter, keep it on the cool side with a minimum of 55°F/13°C.
- **Soil:** Any good potting mix that drains well.
- **Fertilizer:** Feed monthly spring through fall with a balanced liquid fertilizer diluted by half.
- **Propagation:** Division. In spring and summer, divide rhizomes, each with roots and stems attached. Pot in moist potting mix. The rhizomes hold a lot of water, so be careful not to overwater or they'll rot.

67

Rex Begonia

Botanical Name: ***Begonia rex*** **hybrids**

A long-time favourite of house plant lovers, Rex Begonia is grown for its colourful, textured foliage.

These fancy-leafed plants (such as the spiral-leaf, pictured here) produce dramatic, large leaves streaked, veined, or splashed in shades of silver, pink, purple, cream, green, or burgundy.

Tiny, insignificant flowers may grow on tall stems. Pinch them off as soon as you see them to keep the foliage looking its best.

This begonia is rhizomatous, growing from a thick, fleshy rhizome that grows just below the surface of the soil. Repot when the rhizome outgrows the pot, using a shallow pot because of its shallow root system.

Rex begonia can be difficult to grow because of its need for high humidity. Dry, brittle leaves are a symptom of dry air. A terrarium, Wardian case or glass cloche may be just the solution for your humidity-loving begonias.

These fancy-leafed begonias sometimes drop their leaves and become dormant in the winter. If this happens, cut off the withered leaves, stop watering, and enclose the plant in a plastic bag. Keep it at 60°F/16°C until new growth appears, in approximately 6-10 weeks. Then continue with normal care.

Plant Care Tips

- **Origin:** Asia and India
- **Height:** Up to 1 ft (30 cm)
- **Light:** Bright light, but no direct sun which can scorch the leaves. Thrives under fluorescent light.
- **Water:** Keep soil evenly moist at all times, but be careful not to overwater because the rhizomes are prone to rot in soggy soil. Avoid getting water on leaves because they may spot.
- **Humidity:** High humidity. Increase humidity by standing pot on a tray of wet pebbles, or use a room humidifier. Do not mist because this can cause spots to form on leaves.
- **Temperature:** Average room temperatures 65-75°F, 18-24°C.
- **Soil:** African violet potting mix works well.
- **Fertilizer:** Feed every 2 weeks spring through fall with a balanced liquid fertilizer diluted by half.
- **Propagation:** Take leaf cuttings in spring or summer. Cut a healthy, medium-sized leaf with 1-2 in (2.5-5 cm) stem. Poke stem at a 45° angle in moist half-and-half mixture of peat moss and perlite. Enclose the whole thing in a plastic bag to hold in humidity. Keep the cutting in a warm spot (75-80°/24-27°) in indirect light. Leaf cuttings usually root in about 3-4 weeks, but it takes about another 4 weeks for plantlets to form. Pot up each plantlet when it has 3 leaves, and cut away the parent leaf.

68

Rosary Vine

Botanical Name: *Ceropegia linearis woodii*

Whether you call it Rosary Vine or String of Hearts, you'll be captivated by this charming house plant.

Pairs of heart-shaped leaves grow about every 3 in (8 cm) along the slender stems.

Decorative all on their own, the leaves are splotched with a lacey pattern of white on the top and are purple underneath.

Display it in a hanging basket to show off those long, heart-studded vines.

Plant Care Tips

- **Propagate your plant:** Small tubers sometimes grow along the stems, causing the stems to branch out. You can remove the tubers anytime and set them on the surface of the soil to grow more plants in the same pot.
- **Prune it back:** When it starts to look leggy. Propagating the stem cuttings by inserting them back in the soil will give a fuller display that's lush with leaves.
- **Repot in spring:** When it gets crowded, moving to a pot only 1 size bigger. This vining plant grows from 2-inch (5 cm) tubers. Place them on the surface of the soil. Use a

sandy mix and a pot with a drainage hole to avoid soggy soil, which can cause the tubers to rot.

This carefree classic beauty was once an extremely popular indoor plant, but not as common these days. Perhaps it has fallen out of favour because it is *so easy to grow*? Somehow easy-care plants get less respect. If you come across this beautiful succulent vine, buy it. It's long-lived and easy to propagate.

- **Origin:** South Africa
- **Height:** Trails to 3 ft (90 cm) or more
- **Light:** Bright light with some direct sun
- **Water:** Keep the soil lightly moist in spring and summer. Water sparingly in fall and winter. A semi-succulent, this plant is more tolerant of dry soil than wet.
- **Humidity:** Moderate room humidity
- **Temperature:** Normal room temperatures 65-75°F/ 18-24°C
- **Soil:** Mix 1 part good-quality potting mix and 1 part sand or perlite for fast drainage.
- **Fertilizer:** Feed monthly in spring and summer with a balanced liquid fertilizer diluted by half.
- **Propagation:** Take stem tip cuttings and insert cut ends in moist soil. Or, cut off stem tubers and place them on the surface of the soil.

69

Rubber Plant Care

Botanical Name: ***Ficus elastica***

Rubber Plant is a bold evergreen that gets its name from the sticky sap that dries into a low-quality rubber.

It is popular as a house plant, however, because of its large, leathery, glossy leaves that can grow to 8 in (20 cm) long or more—and because it is so easy to grow.

Just like many other plants in the Moraceae family, this one doesn't like to be moved around. Sudden changes in temperature and light may cause it to drop its leaves, although it's not as fussy as its cousin, the weeping fig.

Keep it out of drafts and repot in spring *only* when its roots fill the pot—it likes to be slightly pot-bound. Use a container with drainage holes to prevent overwatering. Never repot a plant that's shedding its leaves, which will make the problem worse.

- **Pruning tip:** The central stem will typically grow straight, without branching. Regular pruning of the growing tip will encourage side branches to form as it grows. You can control its height by simply cutting off the top when it becomes too tall and lanky.

Water regularly to keep it healthy. Leaves that turn yellow and fall off are a sign that it's overwatered. However, it's perfectly natural for older, lower leaves do this.

Few other problems bother this plant. Watch out for sooty mold that can grow on leaves. You can remove it by simply wiping off the affected leaves with mild soapy water. Also check for signs of scale insects and mealybugs that may infest rubber plant. Care should be taken to treat any problems as soon as you notice them.

Keep leaves dust-free and shiny by gently wiping them off with a damp cloth.

Plant Care Tips

- **Origin:** India and Malaysia
- **Height:** Up to 10 ft (3 m)
- **Light:** Bright light, no direct sun.
- **Water:** Keep soil evenly moist. Be careful not to overwater.
- **Humidity:** Average indoor humidity.
- **Temperature:** Normal room temperatures 60-75°F/ 16-24°C.
- **Soil:** Any good potting mix.
- **Fertilizer:** Feed once a month spring through summer with a balanced liquid fertilizer diluted by half.
- **Propagation:** Take stem cuttings in spring. To keep its sticky, white sap from forming a cap on the base of the cutting, place the tip in water for 30 minutes. Remove from the water and dip only the cut surface in rooting hormone. Then, insert it into moist potting mix to root.

70

Sago Palm Tree

Botanical Name: ***Cycas revoluta***

Sago Palm belongs to one of the oldest-known plant families and is one of the most majestic. Despite its common name, it's not really a palm but a Cycad, one of the most primitive of plant families that covered the earth during the age of dinosaurs 200 million years ago.

Real Palm Trees

This tropical plant is extremely slow-growing, but over many years develops a substantial trunk.

Topping the trunk is a rosette of shiny, stiff, narrow fronds arching slightly at their tips. Although the rigid leaves appear tough, they are easily damaged and should be handled carefully.

Sago Palm care is easy if you keep a few things in mind. It doesn't like its feet wet, so keep the soil on the dry side. Give it light every day and fertilize lightly during the growing season.

This plant doesn't really like to be disturbed, so repot only when necessary. Pruning can be done anytime to remove dead fronds.

Sago Palm problems are usually related to watering. Yellowing leaves are often caused by overwatering. Follow the watering instructions below to avoid crown rot. It's almost impossible to treat and plants may not recover. Scale insects are the most common pest. Look over your plant often for scale and treat any infestation immediately with insecticide.

- **Caution:** All parts of this plant are poisonous, especially the seeds. Keep it out of the reach of children and pets that may play with or ingest this plant.

Plant Care Tips

- **Origin:** Tropical Asia
- **Height:** Up to 6 ft (1.8 m) indoors. Can be kept dwarfed by growing it in a small pot. Sago Palm is also popularly grown as a bonsai tree.
- **Light:** Bright light with some direct sun. Turn the pot a quarter turn at least once a week during the growing season. Otherwise, the plant will lean toward the light source.
- **Water:** Take care to water the soil, not the crown of the plant which can lead to crown rot and may kill the plant. Water thoroughly and allow the soil to dry out a bit between waterings, but don't allow it to dry out completely. Water less in winter. Provide good drainage.
- **Humidity:** Requires moist air. Use a humidifier for best results.
- **Temperature:** Normal room temperatures 60-75°F/ 16-24°C
- **Soil:** Cactus mix works well. Or combine 2 parts peat-moss based potting mix and 1 part sharp sand or perlite.
- **Fertilizer:** Feed monthly spring through fall with a liquid fertilizer (such as 18-6-18) diluted by half. Only fertilize when watering to avoid fertilizer burn. A slow-release fertilizer also works well, but I only use half the amount recommended on the package. The leaves will shrivel and dry up when it has been over-fertilized.

- **Propagation:** Seeds take months to germinate and years to grow into a tree. Everything about this plant is slow. Mature plants grow offsets—called *pups*—that can be separated and planted into their own containers.

71

Satin Pothos

Botanical Name: ***Scindapsus pictus*** **'Argyraeus'**

Satin Pothos is just as easy to grow as its relative, golden pothos (*Epipremnum aureum*). Keep it warm and take care not to overwater this house plant. Cold drafts and soggy soil are two things it won't tolerate.

You'll see the best leaf colour and variegation by keeping this pothos plant in bright, indirect light.

This striking tropical plant is fairly new to house plant nurseries, and is garnering a lot of attention.

Big, heart-shaped leaves are dark-green and splashed with silvery gray, giving them a satin sheen. Its compact growth habit makes *Scindapsus pictus* 'Argyraeus' a beautiful hanging basket plant.

- **Pruning tip:** Your plant will benefit from occasional pruning, which helps it to branch out and become fuller. Spring is the best time to cut it back. Use to avoid tearing the stems.

Repot as needed in spring. Keep it in a smallish pot with drainage holes to avoid overwatering, which leads to root rot.

Plant Care Tips

- **Origin:** Southeast Asia
- **Height:** Trails to 3 ft (90 cm) or more.
- **Light:** Bright light, no direct sun.
- **Water:** Water thoroughly and allow the top inch of soil to dry out between waterings. Keep soil barely moist in winter. Yellow leaves are usually a sign of overwatering. Provide good drainage.
- **Humidity:** Moderate-to-high room humidity. Use a room humidifier or a humidity tray in winter.
- **Temperature:** Average to warm 65-85°F, 18-29°C. Don't expose Satin Pothos to temperatures below 65°F/18°C, even for a short time because cold air will damage the foliage.
- **Soil:** Mix 1 part peat moss-based mix and 1 part sand or perlite for good drainage.
- **Fertilizer:** Feed monthly spring through fall with a 20-10-10 liquid fertilizer diluted by half.
- **Propagation:** Take 4 inch (10 cm) tip cuttings in spring or early summer and insert them into moist peat moss based potting mix.

72

Schefflera Plant

Botanical Name: ***Schefflera actinophylla***

Schefflera plant also goes by the name Umbrella Tree.

Its upright branching stems bear horizontal spoke-like leaves that consist of about 8 large, dark-green leaflets. A dwarf variety (*Schefflera arboricola*) is much a smaller and bushier plant. 'Variegata' is a variegated form with green and yellow leaves.

Pruning schefflera may be necessary on large varieties. As the plant ages, it loses its lower leaves, so prune back harshly to stimulate new growth and to keep it full. Pinching off the growing tips will promote branching.

Plants that are allowed to grow tall will need support. Mature plants have aerial roots that can be trained to cling to a moss stick.

Schefflera plant care is easy. Put it in a bright spot, out of direct sun and place the container on a saucer of wet pebbles to increase the humidity around it.

Schefflera doesn't like to be moved around and may drop its leaves if exposed to cold drafts or blasts of hot air from heating vents.

Repot in spring, when roots grow through the drainage holes in the bottom of the pot. Use a heavy pot to prevent toppling—this plant can get top-heavy.

With good care, this beautiful, tropical house plant will live for several years.

Plant Care Tips

- **Origin:** Australia and Pacific Islands
- **Height:** Up to 6 ft (1.8 m)
- **Light:** Bright light, no direct sun. Turn plant occasionally to encourage even growth.
- **Water:** Allow the top inch of soil to dry out between waterings. Yellow leaves are a sign of overwatering. Drooping leaves usually indicate that the soil is too dry.
- **Humidity:** Average indoor humidity. If it gets too dry in the winter, use a room humidifier or mist with water.
- **Temperature:** Average to warm room temperatures 65-75°F/18-24°C.
- **Soil:** Peat moss-based potting mix.
- **Fertilizer:** Feed monthly with a balanced liquid fertilizer diluted by half.
- **Propagation:** Take stem tip cuttings in spring and summer. Can be grown from seeds.

73

Spider Plant or Airplane Plant

Botanical Name: ***Chlorophytum comosum***

Spider Plant is an impressive house plant for beginners. It's easy to care for, tolerates average room conditions, and is easy to propagate.

The slender, arching leaves are dark green with a creamy white stripe. Leaves grow from a central crown and can reach up to 1 ft (30 cm) long. Give this plant plenty of light for the best leaf colour. Plants grown in low light may lose their variegation.

When less than a year old, the plant produces small, white flowers on the tips of wiry, upright stems, called runners.

The runners are soon weighted down with plantlets giving it a spidery appearance.

These plantlets—often called "babies"—are easy to propagate, giving you an ongoing supply of plants. For sure success, choose young, small plantlets for propagating because the larger plantlets are older and will root slowly.

Repot in spring when the plant has outgrown its pot. Move up to a slightly larger pot.

No blooms? These plants like to be slightly root-bound and will flower and produce plantlets best when grown in a smallish container. Also, take it easy on the fertilizer — too much will produce a lot of leaves, but no flowers and plantlets.

Spider plants look best in hanging baskets or on tall stands or pedestals to show off their trailing foliage. Their variegated leaves and graceful, fountain-like growing habit add a beautiful contrast and texture when grouped with other house plants.

Plant Care Tips

- **Origin:** South Pacific and South Africa
- **Height:** Plants grow up to 1 ft (30 cm) tall, with stems trailing to 3 ft (90 cm) in length.
- **Light:** Bright light. Keep plant out of direct sunlight because it can scorch leaves.
- **Water:** Keep soil evenly moist. If your tap water contains fluoride, use distilled or rainwater.
- **Humidity:** Moderate indoor humidity. If the leaves turn brown and crispy, raise the humidity around it.
- **Temperature:** Average room temps 65-75°F/18-24°C suit this tropical plant perfectly. It doesn't like the cold; don't expose it to anything below 50°F/10°C.
- **Soil:** Any good potting mix.
- **Fertilizer:** Feed every 2 weeks spring through summer with a liquid fertilizer diluted by half.
- **Propagation:** Plantlets. Set a small pot filled with damp potting mix next to the plant. Sink a new plantlet into the soil of the small pot, so that the root buds are barely covered. You may need to use a bent paperclip to hold the plantlet in place. It should root in 2-3 weeks. After that time, sever it from the parent plant.

74

Split-Leaf Philodendron

Botanical Name: ***Philodendron bipinnatifidum***

Another dependable house plant from the Araceae family, the split-leaf philodendron also happens to be one of the most captivating.

This stunning philodendron plant is a tree-like shrub. Young plants have sturdy, upright stems, which tend to lie horizontally as the plant ages. They eventually sprawl to become twice as wide as they are tall, so give your house plant plenty of room to spread out.

The foliage is stunning. When young, the glossy, heart-shaped leaves are deeply indented, and become more deeply cut as they grow.

Some varieties of split-leaf philodendron have wavy margins. Gently wipe the leaves with a damp cloth to keep them dust-free and shiny.

The Xanadu Philodendron, shown at left, has a lot of personality. It's a newer cultivar that stays small, making it an ideal indoor plant.

Repot in spring or early summer. Use a container with drainage holes to prevent root rot.

Plant Care Tips

- **Origin:** Brazil
- **Height:** To 4 ft (1.2 m) indoors
- **Light:** Moderate to bright light. No direct sun, which can cause brown scorch marks on the leaves.
- **Water:** Keep soil moist spring through fall. Allow surface to dry out between waterings in winter. Yellow leaves are caused by overwatering.
- **Humidity:** Tolerant of dry air, but likes humidity. Mist foliage occasionally.
- **Temperature:** Average to warm 60-80°F/16-27°C.
- **Soil:** Peat moss-based potting mix.
- **Fertilizer:** Feed monthly spring through fall with a balanced liquid fertilizer diluted by half.
- **Propagation:** Division. Cut through the thick roots with a serrated knife and pot up the plants separately.

75

Staghorn Fern

Botanical Name: ***Platycerium bifurcatum***

Antler-like fronds give staghorn fern its common name. It's also known as elkhorn fern.

This stag horn fern actually has 2 types of fronds. Those at the base of the plant are flat, round and light green, turning brown as they age. Epiphytes in their native habitats, staghorn ferns cling to tree trunks taking in nutrients from fallen leaves and other debris that gets trapped behind these slightly curved fronds.

The second type of fronds grow from the round fronds and can reach up to 3 ft (90 cm) long. These deeply lobed fronds resemble staghorn deer antlers.

You can keep your young plant in a pot, but eventually the round fronds will cover the growing medium making it difficult to water from the top. *Don't saturate these fronds with water because they'll rot easily.* Water pots from below by setting pot in a tray of water for 15 minutes.

- **Transplanting:** When your fern grows bigger, you may want to hang it in a sphagnum moss-lined wire basket or mount it on tree bark or a slab of wood, which is closer to how these ferns grow in their native habitat.

- **Mounting Staghorn Fern:** Place a few handfuls of damp sphagnum moss or orchid mix on a piece of bark or (untreated) wood board. Place the fern over the mound of medium, so that the flat, round basal fronds are touching the board. Use twine, wire or fishing line to firmly hold the fern to the board.

Plant Care Tips

- **Origin:** Australia
- **Height:** Trails up to 3 ft (90 cm)
- **Light:** Stag horns fern grows best in bright, indirect light. Strong summer sun will damage its fronds.
- **Water:** Water thoroughly, allowing medium to dry out between waterings. Water potted plants from below for 15 minutes. For mounted ferns, plunge the root portion into room-temperature water for 15 minutes, then drip-dry. It is better to err on the dry side—mature plants are more tolerant of drought than soggy medium, which can cause root rot.
- **Humidity:** Prefers moist air. Mist leaves often with room-temperature water.
- **Temperature:** Average room temperatures 60-75°F/ 16-24°C
- **Soil:** Sphagnum moss or medium specially made for epiphytes such as bromeliad or orchid mix.
- **Fertilizer:** Feed monthly in summer with a balanced foliar fertilizer or add fertilizer to water and plunge the rootball portion into the water for several minutes.
- **Propagation:** Staghorns produce a large number of offsets—called *pups*—that can be carefully removed and mounted separately. These ferns can also be propagated from spores that grow on the tips of the lobed fronds, however the spores are slow and difficult to propagate and is not practical.

76

Strawberry Begonia Care

Botanical Name: ***Saxifraga stolonifera***

Strawberry Begonia grows in a mound of rounded, scalloped leaves with decorative silvery veins. The leaves are hairy with burgundy-red undersides. Its most charming feature, though, are the long runners with plantlets dangling from the plant. Display it in a hanging basket to show them off.

In its native habitats of China and Japan, *S. stolonifera* grows as a groundcover, spreading quickly by its runners that readily take root. This plant likes cool temperatures, but is frost-tender. Keep it cool and moist, and it makes an easy-care house plant.

Sprays of tiny, white star-shaped flowers on tall stems may appear in summer. You can encourage more flowers by allowing a cool, dry rest for a few weeks in winter.

Strawberry Begonia Care Tips

- **Repot in spring:** Every couple years or when the roots fill the pot. Put it in a hanging pot to show off its trailing plantlets. Use a pot with drainage holes to prevent soggy soil.

- **Brown, crispy leaves?** Dry-looking foliage can be caused by a few things:
- Direct sun can cause leaves to look faded or brown. Keep *Saxifraga stolonifera* out of strong summer sun.
- Crispy, shriveled leaves are often a sign that the air is too dry. Use a pebble tray or a room humidifier to raise the humidity around the plant. Don't mist this plant because the tiny hairs trap water and may cause the leaves to rot.
- Dry soil could also cause dry leaves. Aim to keep the soil lightly moist.

Winter Care

Give this evergreen plant a dry, cool rest in winter. Keep it in a cool (50-55°F/10-13°C) place, and water sparingly, but don't allow the soil to dry out. It'll suffer in the dry air caused by central heating. Use a humidity tray or room humidifier, if necessary to raise the moisture in the air around it. Watch for an invasion of spider mites that are attracted to dry conditions.

Plant Care Tips

- **Origin:** East Asia.
- **Height:** Up to 8 in (20 cm); runners trail to 12 in (30 cm) or more.
- **Light:** Bright light year-round. Some direct morning sun is fine, but shade from strong sun, which can cause leaves to fade.
- **Water:** Water thoroughly and allow the top inch (2.5 cm) of soil to dry between waterings. Water less in winter, when growth is slower. Overwatering can lead to root rot or crown rot and may cause fungus.
- **Humidity:** Moderate humidity. Use a humidity tray if air is dry.
- **Temperature:** Cool to average room temperatures 50-75°F/10-24°C.

- **Soil:** Any good potting mix.
- **Fertilizer:** Feed monthly in spring and summer with a balanced liquid fertilizer diluted by half.
- **Propagation:** Propagating is easy to do from runners. Place small pots around the parent plant. Leave the runners attached and, using a bent paper clip, hold plantlets down into moist potting mix. The plantlets will quickly form roots. After 3 weeks, you can cut the runners to detach them from the parent plant.

77

Sundew Plant

If you like unusual plants, you'll want to add Sundew Plant to your collection. Its other-worldly foliage and strange eating habits make it a fascinating carnivorous plant for the collector.

Sundew features long leaves that grow in a rosette. Round, disk-like leaves are covered with red glandular hairs—or tentacles—that secrete a sticky juice, luring flies and other insects.

Fooled into mistaking that glistening liquid for nectar, bugs are attracted to them. As soon as the bugs land, they're stuck. Then the action starts: As the insect struggles, the leaf seems to gobble it, holding the bug with its tentacles and smothering it. Sundews produce a digestive enzyme that breaks down protein from the insect so that it can be absorbed by the plant.

You can expect small, white flowers to appear in summer, rising above the rosette on tall stems. Each flower is short-lived, but you'll get dozens of blooms from healthy plants during the growing season. Wait for flowers to dry and you can collect their seeds—they're viable and ready to sow for more Sundews.

What Sundews Want

Sundew Plant loves lots of moisture and flies. Give it what it wants and you'll watch it grow quickly, producing more leaves and flowers.

Feed me, Seymour

Sundews need to eat to survive and grow. They have shallow root systems and get all their nourishment from the insects they capture. Since your carnivorous plant is unlikely to catch flies or other insects in the house, you'll want to feed it. (Isn't that the fun of having this plant, anyway?)

Native to bogs and marshes, this carnivorous plant prefers higher humidity than is usually found in a home. It's a good idea to place it in a terrarium or Wardian case to maintain humidity around it.

Give it a Winter Rest

Sundews are perennials that go dormant in winter and need a cool rest. Keep your plant moist and cool during dormancy, with temperatures between 32-50°F/1-10°C (it will tolerate some frost). Moving it to a garage for the winter may be ideal, just be sure it gets some light.

Dying leaves?

It is normal for dropped leaves during the winter rest, and Sundew Plant will grow new leaves in spring and summer. Hot temperatures can cause dormancy, so if this happens, don't give up on it. With good care, it should bounce back. This is a tempermental plant that doesn't like extreme heat, direct sunlight or dry conditions, so if it dies don't feel badly. It's a good idea to save the seeds, so you'll have more plants.

Plant Care Tips

- **Origin:** North America, Northern Europe and North Asia
- **Height:** Up to 3 in (8 cm)
- **Light:** Bright indirect light
- **Water:** Aim to keep the potting medium evenly moist. Never let it dry out completely.

- **Humidity:** Moderate to high. If the relative humidity drops below 50 per cent, you'll want to raise the humidity for your plant.
- **Temperature:** Cool to average room temperatures 60-75ºF/16-24ºC; In winter, a cold rest is needed 32-50ºF/1-10ºC. It will tolerate a little frost. High heat may cause dormancy, so it's best to maintain normal room temps for it.
- **Soil:** Live sphagnum moss or a half-and-half mix of peat moss and horticultural sand
- **Fertilizer:** Don't fertilize because it will burn the roots and may kill the plant. Since sundews are unlikely to catch insects in the house, you can feed it dead flies spring through fall. *Don't* use flies that have been exposed to insecticide because it will damage the plant.
- **Propagation:** Seeds or division. Collect seeds from flowers that have dried and sow them in peat moss (kept moist at all times). Place the pots in a warm window or under fluorescent lights. Seeds germinate in about 2-4 weeks. To divide, separate new rosettes that form around the parent plant.

78

Swedish Ivy

Botanical Name: *Plectranthus* species

Swedish ivy house plants are ideal for beginners. Nearly foolproof, this is one of the easiest types of ivy to grow indoors. In fact, it needs little attention to thrive.

This bushy plant has thick stems that grow upright at first, then trail over the sides of a container. Put it in a hanging basket to show off its thickly leaved cascading stems.

Swedish ivy has rounded leaves that are deeply veined with scalloped edges. *P. australis* is a variety with solid green foliage. The variegated types are more commonly grown as house plants. You can expect pale lavender or white flowers to appear in spring or summer, but they're not nearly as showy as the foliage.

Plant Care Tips

- **Keep it moist, not soggy:** This plant grows best with evenly moist soil during the growing season. Take care not to allow the soil to become soggy, which can cause root rot. If your plant wilts despite regular watering, it is probably suffering from root rot. If this happens, take a few stem cuttings from the healthiest stems and propagate them. Get rid of the parent plant — it won't recover. Cut back on water in the winter, when growth has slowed. But don't allow it to dry out completely.

- **Pinch and prune:** This vigorous grower needs regular pruning to keep it in shape. After the flowers fade, pinch back stem tips to encourage branching. You'll get a fuller, bushier plant this way. Propagate the stem tips, if you like. They'll root easily and you'll have new plants. You can prune your plant back by as much as half at a time — you won't hurt this robust plant at all.
- **Origin:** Northern Australia, Pacific Islands
- **Height:** To 3 ft (90 cm)
- **Light:** Bright, indirect light. Some morning sun is fine.
- **Water:** Keep soil moist spring through fall when plant is actively growing. Water sparingly in winter.
- **Humidity:** Moderate humidity. This plant loves to be misted with room-temperature water.
- **Temperature:** Average room temperatures (60-75°F/ 16-24°C) year-round.
- **Soil:** Peat moss-based potting mix.
- **Fertilizer:** Feed monthly spring through fall with a balanced liquid fertilizer diluted by half. Do not feed in winter.
- **Propagation:** Take stem cuttings in spring or summer. They'll root easily in water or moist potting mix.

79

Sweet Potato Vine

Botanical Name: ***Ipomoea batatas***

Mounds of dense, colourful foliage make sweet potato vine a favourite ornamental. Sweet potato plants are also fast-growing and practically care-free.

Sweet potato leaves offer bold colour from spring through fall. You don't need to overwinter—treat this vine as an annual.

In addition to the garden-variety green foliage, you'll find an abundance of new cultivars with striking leaf shapes, in a stunning range of colours: lime green, golden yellow, coppery gold with a tinge of red, and rich, purplish-black.

There is one draw-back with this vigorous vine . . . it has a tendency to take over any space available. It will crowd other plants if you let it. Don't be afraid to cut mature sweet potato vines back as much as needed to keep it under control. And, don't throw away those cuttings, either. They'll root easily if you poke them into moist soil.

Wondering where to grow sweet potato plant? Its trailing habit makes it ideal for a warm, sunny windowsill. Plant it in a hanging basket—or a windowbox—and let its lush vines spill over the side. Or, use it as an underplanting for tall flowers outdoors.

Allow it to climb a trellis, if you want. This twining climber makes a gorgeous backdrop for tall, upright plants in contrasting colours.

Plant Care Tips

- **Origin:** Central America
- **Height:** Up to 12 in (30 cm) tall; will spread or trail several ft if not cut back.
- **Light:** Moderate to bright light. Will tolerate some direct sunlight.
- **Water:** Keep soil evenly moist at all times. This fast-growing vine is thirsty and dries out quickly in a container, so check it often. Use a container with drainage holes to prevent soggy soil.
- **Humidity:** Moderate to high humidity
- **Temperature:** Average to warm room temperatures (65-80°F/18-27°C). Wait till it's warm if you move it outside; this tender vine won't tolerate frost.
- **Soil:** Any good potting mix.
- **Fertilizer:** Feed monthly in spring and summer with a balanced liquid fertilizer diluted by half.
- **Propagation:** Stem tip cuttings, root cuttings, or slips (sprouts). Can be started from sweet potatoes. Place a whole sweet potato in a jar with a little water and it will dependably grow roots and sprout slips. Break off sweet potato slips when they are about 6 in (15 cm) and pot them in moist potting mix. They'll take root in a few weeks.

80

Swiss Cheese Plant

Botanical Name: ***Monstera deliciosa***

Lush and bold, Swiss Cheese Plant makes a good accent if you have the space.

Over several years it can grow to 10 ft (3 m) tall and its dramatic, perforated leaves to 12 inches (30 cm) long or more, so it needs a bit of elbow room.

This handsome foliage plant is a climber in the wild, scrambling up large trees, anchoring itself with thick aerial roots which also take in moisture and nutrients. You can tuck aerial roots that emerge near its base into the soil and train others to climb a moss pole.

Keep Leaves Clean

Gently wipe off leaves to keep them dust-free and shiny.

Young plants have smooth leaves. But as it matures, the leaves develop deeply cut edges and wide slits.

In its native jungle habitat, the slashes, holes and cuts in the large leaves help the plant to withstand strong winds and torrential downpours.

- **Caution:** The leaves of Swiss Cheese Plant are poisonous and can cause severe burning in the mouth if eaten. They can also cause skin irritation, so I'd recommend wearing gloves when handling this plant.

Repot in spring when roots have filled the pot. Use a pot with drainage holes to prevent overwatering.

Plant Care Tips

- **Origin:** Southern Mexico and Guatemala
- **Height:** Up to 10 ft (3 m) tall.
- **Light:** Bright light, no direct sun. If leaves on mature plants grow without holes or slits, give the plant more light.
- **Water:** Water thoroughly and allow the top inch of soil to dry out between waterings. Keep soil barely moist in winter. Yellowing lower leaves are usually a sign of overwatering. Provide good drainage.
- **Humidity:** Normal room humidity.
- **Temperature:** Average to warm 65-85°F/18-29°C
- **Soil:** Mix 1 part peat moss-based mix and 1 part sand or perlite for good drainage.
- **Fertilizer:** Feed every 2 weeks spring through fall with a balanced liquid fertilizer diluted by half. Feed monthly in winter.
- **Propagation:** Take growing tip cuttings of a mature plant in spring and insert them into moist peat moss based potting mix.

81

Ti Plant Hawaiian

Botanical Name: ***Cordyline terminalis***

Ti plant makes a stunning accent, lending a colourful, tropical feel to a sunny room.

Its broad leaves grow up to 2 ft (60 cm) long and are carried on upright stems that emerge from a narrow, central stalk. As the plant grows, it naturally drops its lower leaves, becoming more tree-like with a trunk topped with a cluster of colourful foliage.

Some ti plants have solid green leaves, but the most popular house plants include varieties with red, pink, cream, orange or copper variegation. In the wild, plants will produce pink or yellow flower spikes, but don't expect them when grown indoors.

Clean Leaves

Wipe leaves gently with a damp cloth or spray with a fine mist of room-temperature water to keep them clean. Cleaning the leaves has another advantage — it helps to prevent spider mites that love dry conditions.

Raise the Humidity

This tropical native prefers moist air, especially in the hot summer months. Dry air will cause leaf tips to turn brown.

Keep ti plant away from drafts and heat/AC vents. A room humidifier works best to add humidity around your cordyline plant. It also loves to be misted.

Repot Young Plants

In spring when their roots have filled the container. Move it to a pot only one size larger. Be sure to use a pot with a drainage hole to prevent root rot. Older, larger ti plants can be top-dressed instead.

- **Pruning tip:** You can control the plant's height by cutting it back. New branches often grow from the base of the plant after pruning. Use sharp pruners to avoid tearing the stems.

Plant Care Tips

- **Origin:** Southeast Asia, Pacific Islands
- **Height:** 3-5 ft (90 cm-1.5 m) indoors
- **Light:** Bright, indirect light. Leaves that lose their colour and variegation aren't getting enough light.
- **Water:** Keep soil evenly moist spring through fall. In winter, allow the top inch (2.5 cm) to dry out between waterings. Use rainwater to avoid adding fluoride and chlorine that's often present in tap water. If that's not practical, allow tap water to sit for 24 hours so that the chemicals in it will dissipate.
- **Humidity:** Moderate to high humidity
- **Temperature:** Average to warm 60-85°F/16-29°C.
- **Soil:** Peat moss-based potting mix.
- **Fertilizer:** Spring through fall, feed every 2 weeks with a balanced fertilizer diluted by half. Choose one that includes micronutrients — a magnesium deficiency will cause leaves to turn yellow. In winter, feed monthly.
- **Propagation:** These are easy to grow from cuttings. Take 4 in (10 cm) stem tip cuttings in spring and root them in moist potting mix. Keep young plants warm and humid.

82

Tradescantia pallida - Purple Heart Plant

Botanical Name: ***Tradescantia pallida***

If you've never grown Purple Heart Plant, you may want tc add it to your collection. It's a relative of the Wandering Jew plant, and you'll find it's just as easy to grow.

Bunches of rich purple, lance-shaped leaves make this a beautiful house plant year-round. Pot it in a small decorative container for an eye-catching table accent. Or, hang it in a basket and let the long, sprawling stems cascade over the side.

In summer, you can expect small, pink 3-petaled flowers to bloom. They grow in the leaf axils, making a stunning contrast to the dark foliage.

Plant Care Tips

- **Let the sun shine in:** Grow your plant in bright light year-round for good foliage colour. It will grow in lower light, but the leaves will be more green than purple. Give it some direct sun, but shade it from noonday sun in summer to avoid scorching its leaves.
- **Pinch your plant:** Pinching off new stem tips will promote branching and keep *Tradescantia pallida* compact.

Don't toss out those cuttings — you can easily propagate them for more plants.

- **Repot in spring:** Move up to a pot only 1 size larger to give it a little room to grow. Use a pot with drainage holes to prevent soggy soil, which leads to root rot.
- **Origin:** Mexico
- **Height:** Trails to 2 ft (60 cm)
- **Light:** Bright light. Some direct sun is fine, but keep your plant shaded from strong summer sun.
- **Water:** Water thoroughly, then allow the top 1 in (2.5 cm) to dry out between waterings.
- **Humidity:** Average room humidity.
- **Temperature:** Average to warm room temperatures (65-80°F/18-27°C) suit this plant year-round. Purple heart tolerates varying temperatures with a minimum of 50°F/10°C in winter.
- **Soil:** Peat moss-based potting mix.
- **Fertilizer:** Feed monthly in spring and summer with a balanced (10-10-10) liquid fertilizer diluted by half.
- **Propagation:** Take 4 in (10 cm) stem tip cuttings in spring or early summer. They'll root easily in moist potting mix.

83

Venus Fly Trap

Botanical Name: ***Dionaea muscipula***

In its native habitat, the Venus Fly Trap plant grows in bogs where it is unable to get the nutrients it needs from the soil. Therefore, it has developed a way to feed from the insects it traps in its leaves.

Feed Me?

This bug-munching plant makes food by photosynthesis, so feeding it insects is not critical for its survival. But, isn't that the fun of growing this captivating house plant?

This unusual, carnivorous plant grows in a rosette of broad-winged stems, each with 2 rounded leaves that turn red inside when exposed to sunlight.

The leaves are hinged in the middle by a midrib and fringed with interlocking "teeth" to hold in its prey.

Inside each leaf are a few sensitive hairs that when touched trigger the leaves to snap shut. The action is quick, and the traps may stay closed for as long as 2 weeks. Then they open again, ready for the next victim. *Heh, heh.*

Although it's fascinating to watch, try not to get overzealous. It's not a good idea to trigger them too often because the traps will stop responding after only a few times.

Venus Flytrap for Sale

Clusters of white flowers may appear in spring. Pick off the flower stems as soon as you see them because they will use the plant's energy to flower instead of growing traps.

Venus Fly Trap is a perennial plant that can be kept from year to year. Understanding its needs for moisture and light will keep it healthy. Never allow the potting medium to dry out, which can be fatal. Also maintain high humidity. Covering the plant with a glass cloche is the most practical way to retain humidity around it.

D. muscipula will go dormant in winter when a cool rest is needed. Keep it barely moist and cool during dormancy, with temperatures between 32-50°F/1-10°C. Moving it to a garage for the winter may be ideal...just be sure it gets some sunlight and the temps don't drop below freezing.

Plant Care Tips

- **Origin:** North and South Carolina
- **Height:** 3-10 in (8-25 cm)
- **Light:** Good light is vital to this plant's health. Bright light with 4 hours of direct sun a day is ideal. Sunlight is more important than feeding the plant because it makes most of its food through photosynthesis.
- **Water:** Keep soil evenly moist spring through fall. In winter, give it just enough water to keep from drying out completely. This plant is sensitive to chemicals in tap water, so it's a good idea to use only distilled or rain water.
- **Humidity:** Requires moist air. Grows best in a terrarium.
- **Temperature:** Normal room temperatures 60-75°F/ 16-24°C; In winter, a near-freezing dormancy period is needed 32-50°F/1-10°C
- **Soil:** Use nutrient-poor soil because rich potting mix will harm its roots. You can use all sphagnum moss or mix 1 part peat moss with 1 part perlite.

- **Fertilizer:** Don't fertilize. Fertilizer will burn the roots and may kill the plant. Since it is unlikely to catch insects in the house, you can feed it dead flies occasionally in spring and summer. *Don't* use flies that have been exposed to insecticide because it will harm the plant.
- **Propagation:** Divide rhizomes in spring; can be grown from seed.

84

Wandering Jew

Botanical Name: ***Tradescantia albiflora***

Best known as a hanging plant, the Wandering Jew house plant is easy and fast-growing. Its long, fleshy stems are densely covered with lance-shaped leaves that are about 2 in (5 cm) long.

A similar plant goes by the same common name: *Zebrina pendula* has deep green to purple leaves with two broad bands of silver, and purple undersides. It has the same growing habits and requires the same care.

- **Pinch and prune:** Pinch stems back often to encourage branching and to keep the plant from getting too leggy. The best time to prune is in spring and summer, during the growing season. You can easily propagate the stem cuttings for more plants.
- **Pruning tip:** Always prune above a leaf node (the place where a leaf is attached to the stem). Cuts made here will cause the stem to branch out for a fuller, bushier plant.
- **Give it light:** Long spaces between leaves are caused by too little light. Pinch off leggy stems and move your plant to a brighter spot. Leaves will also lose their variegation if they don't get enough light.

Plant Care Tips

- **Origin:** South America
- **Height:** Trailing stems can grow to 2 ft (60 cm) or more.
- **Light:** Bright, indirect light.
- **Water:** Keep soil evenly moist in the growing season, slightly drier in winter.
- **Humidity:** Moderate humidity. If leaf tips turn brown, the air is too dry. Increase moisture by using a humidifier or by misting the plant occasionally.
- **Temperature:** Average room temperatures 60-75°F/ 16-24°C.
- **Soil:** Peat moss based mix.
- **Fertilizer:** Feed every 2 weeks spring through fall with 10-10-10 liquid fertilizer diluted by half. Too much fertilizer can cause the leaves to lose their variegation.
- **Propagation:** Easy to propagate from stem tip cuttings. Take 3 in (7.5 cm) cuttings in spring or summer and place in moist soil. Cuttings will root in about 3 weeks.

85

Weeping Fig

Botanical Name: ***Ficus benjamina***

Weeping fig is the most popular indoor tree from the Moraceae family.

Its branches droop downward from woody stems, covered with glossy, pointed 2-4 in (5-10 cm) leaves which become darker green as the plant ages. Growers sometimes braid its trunks for a decorative topiary look.

These ficus trees are slow-growing, but can grow to 10 ft indoors. Dwarf varieties only reach 3 ft (90 cm) tall. You can prune tall branches to control the plant's height.

- **Watering tip:** Weeping fig tree is sensitive to chlorine, fluoride, and other chemicals often found in tap water, as well as the salt in softened water. Use only distilled or filtered water, or allow tap water to sit overnight so the chemicals will dissipate.
- **This is a plant that doesn't like change:** Place your ficus in bright, indirect light and leave it there. It's known to drop its leaves when moved around. Keep it away from drafts. Blasts of hot or cold air from doorways or vents will also cause leaf drop. If this happens, don't worry. With good care it will grow new leaves in spring and summer.

In early fall, expect it to drop quite a few leaves. This is normal. You can help prevent the tree from losing too many leaves by misting it to increase humidity. Also, don't be tempted to overwater a shedding plant, which makes the problem worse.

Weeping fig is a long-lived house plant. Give it what it wants and you'll enjoy it for many, many years.

Plant Care Tips

- **Origin:** Southeast Asia and Northern Australia
- **Height:** Up to 10 ft (3 m)
- **Light:** Bright light
- **Water:** Water thoroughly, then allow to dry out slightly between waterings. This plant will not tolerate soggy soil. Keep soil slightly drier in winter, when light levels are lower.
- **Humidity:** High humidity.
- **Temperature:** Average room temperatures 60-75°F/ 16-24°C.
- **Soil:** Soilless potting mix or any that drains well.
- **Fertilizer:** Feed once a month spring through fall with a balanced liquid fertilizer diluted by half.
- **Propagation:** Take tip cuttings in spring.

86

Windmill Palm Tree

Botanical Name: ***Trachycarpus fortunei***

Windmill palm tree is one of the most adaptable palms you can grow. This tree is a giant in its native habitat, but only reaches 6-8 ft when grown in a container indoors. Slow-growing, it will take this indoor palm plant several years to reach this height.

The whorl of fan-shaped fronds make it a stunning decorative accent tree. Young fronds have pleated leaflets that gradually open into widely spaced fans.

As the palm grows, it develops a thick trunk which is covered with coarse brown fibers.

Light Tip

Moving your palm outdoors? Make the move a gradual one. Palms that go into hot, direct summer sun then back to indirect light indoors may drop their leaflets.

Shed Some Light

Give this palm as much light as you can. Move it outdoors for the summer, if you want. Just be sure to keep it protected from strong winds, which can damage the fronds. A sheltered porch or patio is ideal.

Repot in Spring

Every 2-3 years or as needed, moving it to a pot 1 size larger. Older plants that are too big to repot can be top-dressed instead by replacing the top couple inches of soil. Crowding roots helps to control its size. Use a heavy container to prevent it from toppling because this palm gets top-heavy.

Brown leaf tips are often caused by sporadic watering, low humidity or a build-up of chemicals in tap water and fertilizers. It's a good idea to water palms with distilled, filtered or rain water.

Palms are sensitive to fluoride and chlorine often found in tap water, and salts from fertilizer. You can get rid of these impurities in the soil by flushing the container. It's easy to do: Pour lots of water over the soil so that the water comes out the drainage holes. Repeat the process a couple more times, then empty the drainage tray.

Plant Care Tips

- **Origin:** Southeast Asia
- **Height:** Up to 8 ft (2.4 m) indoors
- **Light:** Bright light with plenty of direct sun.
- **Water:** Keep soil moist spring through summer and barely moist in fall and winter.
- **Humidity:** Moderate humidity. Mist regularly in winter if the relative humidity drops below 50 per cent.
- **Temperature:** Average room temperature 65-75°F/18-24°C year-round. This is one of the few "indoor palms" that can tolerate cold. Windmill palm loves warmth, but will tolerate a minimum of 40°F/4°C.
- **Soil:** Use a peaty mix that drains well. Mix 1 part sand to 3 parts African violet mix.
- **Fertilizer:** Feed once in spring and again in summer with a time-release fertilizer. Rose fertilizer works well because it provides the micronutrients this palm needs. A shortage of magnesium will cause yellow spots on the leaflets.
- **Propagation:** Plants can be grown from seeds, but seedlings are slow-growing and you'll wait several years for them to grow into trees.

87

Zebra Plant

Botanical Name: ***Aphelandra squarrosa***

Zebra Plant has exotic, emerald green leaves with dramatic white veins so striking, it is grown for its foliage.

The plume of bright yellow flowers emerging from golden bracts in fall are an added attraction. The flowers will only last a few days, but the bracts will stay for about 6 weeks.

Cut off the bracts after they deteriorate. *Aphelandra squarrosa* will often bloom a second time during the year when given enough light.

Zebra Plants are often forced into bloom in winter and sold while they're flowering. However, they naturally bloom in spring and fall.

Unlike some flowering plants, these tropicals are triggered into bloom by the intensity of light rather than day length. Put your plant in a bright location, but keep it out of direct sunlight or you may see its leaves curl up or look wrinkled.

Pruning Tip

Plants will get leggy over time. Plants that have flowered should be cut down in spring. Cut the main stem, leaving a pair of its lower leaves.

In the wild, it thrives in the high humidity and frequent downpours of the rain forest. It will thrive indoors, too, as long as its need for high humidity is met. A room humidifier is the most effective way to increase moisture in the air. Or, you can stand the pot on a tray of wet pebbles to raise humidity around the plant.

Zebra plant prefers to be slightly pot-bound and blooms best this way. Keep it in a smallish pot. Repot in spring when needed to refresh the soil.

Wipe leaves often with a damp cloth to keep them glossy and dust-free.

Plant Care Tips

- **Origin:** Brazil
- **Height:** 1-2 ft (30-60 cm)
- **Light:** Bright light but no direct sun. Wrinkled or curled leaves indicate it is getting too much light.
- **Water:** Keep soil evenly moist year-round. Dry soil will cause leaves to wilt or drop off.
- **Humidity:** High humidity
- **Temperature:** Warm 65-80°F/18-27°C.
- **Soil:** Peat moss based potting mix or African violet mix.
- **Fertilizer:** Feed monthly spring and summer with a balanced liquid fertilizer diluted by half.
- **Propagation:** Take 3-inch (7.5 cm) stem tip cuttings in spring or summer. Cut the stem just below a *node* — the place where a leaf is attached to the main stem. Dip cut ends in rooting powder then insert them in seed starting mix or perlite. Enclose the potted cuttings in clear plastic or use a glass cloche to hold in humidity. Set the covered cuttings where they'll get indirect light. Water when the potting medium appears to dry out. After 3 weeks, you can remove the covering. Gradually expose the cuttings to more light. You should see new growth in about 6 weeks.

88

ZZ Plant

Botanical Name: ***Zamioculcas zamiifolia***

ZZ Plant has become increasingly popular in recent years and I believe it deserves all the attention it's been getting.

The Aroid family has given us more dependable house plants than any other group and *Zamioculcas zamiifolia* is no exception. This is a worthwhile house plant to add to your collection.

ZZ makes a great room accent and practically thrives on neglect. This easy-going house plant is forgiving if you forget to water, tolerates low light, and rarely needs fertilized. Want more? It also seems to shrug off pests.

Growing from rhizomes, it has thick, upright stems bearing narrow, dark-green glossy leaves. Keep the leaves clean by gently wiping them with a damp cloth. *Don't use leaf shine products,* which can damage the plant.

Small, insignificant flowers — consisting of a spadix surrounded by a spathe — may appear at the base of plants in summer, although ZZs rarely flower indoors.

A slow-grower indoors, ZZ plant rarely needs repotted. Keep it in a small pot (no more than 2 in (5 cm) wider than the old pot) with drainage holes to prevent root rot.

Overwatering ZZ is a sure-fire way to kill it. To avoid soggy soil, use a fast-draining mix. You can add sand or perlite to a potting mix or use a cactus mix.

- **Watering Tip:** Despite being drought-tolerant, your ZZ will be healthiest with regular watering. Water thoroughly then allow it to dry out a bit before watering again.
- **Caution:** All parts of this plant are poisonous. Keep it away from children and pets who may play with or ingest this plant.

Plant Care Tips

- **Origin:** East Africa
- **Height:** Slow-growing, but can reach up to 3 ft (90 cm) indoors. It grows much taller in its native habitat.
- **Light:** Bright to low light. Keep it out of direct sunlight which can scorch its leaves.
- **Water:** Water thoroughly and allow the top 2 in (5 cm) of soil to dry out between waterings. Soggy soil will cause the rhizomes to rot.
- **Humidity:** Average indoor humidity.
- **Temperature:** Average room temperatures 60-75°F/ 16-24°C
- **Soil:** Fast-draining medium works best to avoid root rot. Mix 1 part good-quality all-purpose potting mix and 1 part sharp sand or perlite. Cactus mix works well, too.
- **Fertilizer:** Feed 4 times a year with a balanced liquid fertilizer diluted by half.
- **Propagation:** Division of rhizomes. Leaf cuttings can be propagated. But be patient — the cuttings can take several months to grow.

Index